eight paths to forgiveness

The Seattle School
2510 Elliott Ave.
Seattle, WA 98121
theseattleschool.edu

December 1998

To Sandy and Liz,

with deep appreciation for your

creative and gracious ministry

among us in Wenatchee

With my love,

Bob

eight paths to forgiveness

ROBERT BRIZEE

Chalice Press
St. Louis, Missouri

All scripture quotations, unless otherwise indicated, are from the *New Revised Standard Version Bible,* copyright 1989, Division of Christian Education of the National Council of the Churches of Christ in the USA. Used by permission.

Art direction: Lynne Condellone

Interior design: Elizabeth Wright

This book is printed on acid-free, recycled paper.

Visit Chalice Press on the World Wide Web at
www.chalicepress.com

10 9 8 7 6 5 4 3 2 1   98 99 00 01 02 03

Library of Congress Cataloging–in–Publication Data

Brizee, Robert
    Eight paths to forgiveness/ by Robert Brizee.
      p.   cm.
    Includes index.
    ISBN 0-8272-0811-1
    1. Forgiveness—Religious aspects—Christianity. 2. Theodicy.
3. Presence of God. 4. Process theology. I. Title
BV4647.F55B75   1998   98–31359
234'.5—dc21   CIP

Printed in the United States of America

Contents

Preface

I wrote this book in an effort to help people. In my forty years of counseling I have heard too many hurting persons blocked from healing by the impossibility of forgiving. Starting with their understanding of forgiveness, they had nowhere to go.

It is my conviction that a new vision of God leads to new forms of forgiveness. Those who were blocked may now be able to forgive and live both fully and freely.

Beginning with this vision, I chose eight of the most difficult human situations I could imagine. Each of the eight situations is unique and particular, yet represents a class of offenses. I hope they exhibit a variety of differences so that the concept of forgiveness will be fully stretched and tested.

I asked: How might one caught in this situation forgive if he or she embraced this understanding of God? Naturally, the answers look different. There are many paths to forgiveness, depending upon one's painful situation.

If some of the answers look different from those proposed elsewhere, that is to be expected. Starting with a new understanding of how God graces all persons will lead to differing ways of forgiving. Of all the varied ways suggested today about how to go about forgiveness, mine is an additional choice.

The new vision is offered first, followed by eight situations that are based on reality blended with my imagination. Each is followed by a meditation that is intended to bring that situation to a more personal level. Each meditation is to be only the beginning brush stroke on the canvas, thereby longing to be revised by the reader to be more relevant to each person's particular situation.

Following the eight situations, a flight of imagination proposes that the final process of forgiveness occurs in God's heavenly community. Finally, a brief afterword endeavors to sum up the central characteristics of the vision that underlies the eight paths to forgiveness.

It is my hope that the words that I have crafted will offer new pathways to persons desperately seeking healing.

I am indebted to two centers of learning that informed me in this endeavor: Michigan State University, where I was mentored in the gift of listening, and Claremont School of Theology, where I was encouraged to embrace a world vision. I could not have developed the imagination necessary for this work without both.

I am grateful to the Center for Process Studies and the Process and Faith program of that Center for the encouragement that I have received to crystallize and translate my theological vision. Dr. John B. Cobb, Jr., Dr. William A. Beardslee, Dr. Mary Elizabeth Mullino Moore, and Dr. Marjorie Hewitt Suchocki have been especially important mentors.

In my home community I am indebted to my pastor, Dr. Sanford Brown, who challenges my imagination weekly through awesome sermons; my spouse, Adrienne Brizee, who accompanies me in my development of each emerging creative thought; and my former pastor, Dr. Mary Ann Swenson, now bishop of the Denver area of the United Methodist Church, who encouraged and presently promotes my earlier works and offered mentoring on this manuscript.

To Dr. David Polk, my former classmate at Claremont, now editor-in-chief of Chalice Press, I offer my gratitude for his excited response to the proposal of this work on forgiveness.

It is with deep pleasure that I dedicate this book to two special persons in my life:

Adrienne Brizee

Mary Ann Swenson

A New Vision of God

"I know I let you down. I'm really sorry!"

"It's all right. No problem."

We have before us the simplest model of forgiveness, which works for many situations, but not for more complex struggles. Consider with me the following:

A woman leaves her marriage, breaking her wedding vows. Her husband, crying out, "But she broke her vow," is filled with disbelief, hurt, and vengefulness. She is neither remorseful nor asking for forgiveness, but is rather relieved. He is utterly baffled about what forgiveness means here.

A woman is left black and blue by her husband's beating. She is justly offended and enraged. In contrast, he believes she pushed him into doing it. Later, he moves into remorse and sadness, promising that it will never happen again and beginning his familiar cycle of abuse. She is torn between her conviction of what her faith tells her to do and what she cannot once again do.

A young woman becomes aware belatedly that her stepfather sexually abused her over a period of her childhood years. The man, when finally confronted by her, adamantly denies that he ever touched her. Efforts to convince him are met by angry denials. She ponders how one is to forgive someone who denies any wrongdoing.

The women had not seen their husbands and sons since that night. Only as the international agencies began the grisly task of sifting through what appeared to be mass graves did the Bosnian women grasp the terrible ending. Could anything but hatred and tears, leading to vowed vengeance, fill their lives?

The production workers are shocked to learn that the company plans to shut down an entire section of the juice processing plant. Three generations of their families have labored here, and the community has depended on their income for its survival. They face not a human offender but an idea, "the bottom line of profit," as they struggle toward some form of forgiveness.

Two young persons are swept away by a rain-swollen river, their bodies to be recovered only days later. The parents of the youths experience deep grief, at the same time radically questioning a God who would allow this tragedy to occur. Forgiving God seems impossible to them.

Three children start a small fire on a hillside to heat their cocoa. By the end of the day thirty-two homes have burned to the ground. The losses in dollars are mammoth, but the irreplaceable losses in possessions are heart breaking. It was an accident, it was unintentional; yet the profound losses are starkly unbelievable. Sifting through the ashes with a heavy heart, a homeowner wonders whether shock, grief, loss, and unfairness will ever give way to acceptance and forgiveness.

The young man dozed off while driving home from a day in the sun at the lake, allowing his car to veer across the center line and smash head-on into a van carrying a family of seven. The carnage of the family was strewn on the highway among the burning debris, while he and the passenger in his car were hospitalized with minor injuries. The driver might well remain in a state of self-blame, constantly reliving that costly lapse of awareness, or he may find some way toward self-forgiveness.

It is my conviction that forgiveness can bring healing to each of these tragic events, but not by the simple model of apologizing we learned as children: "Say you're sorry." "Now, kiss and make up." I am suggesting, rather, that there are a number of paths to forgiveness, each of which or a combination of which is most helpful in particular situations. My aim is to present this wide variety of situations to illustrate the paths to forgiveness.

Having introduced the tearing and tragic situations, it is now time to present a perspective from which they will be viewed. Truly, each of these situations is open to a variety of interpretations leading to differing ways of reaching for wholeness.

As I gaze upon my book shelf I see twenty books that address the subject of forgiveness, and I can readily place my hands on over one hundred articles on forgiveness in the file drawer nearby. There is no doubt that many viewpoints exist on this vital subject. My perspective will be one among many. It will contrast with some, overlap with others; but its uniqueness will be its starting point.

My perspective can be stated simply: A new vision of God leads to new paths to forgiveness. I am proposing that the process of forgiveness starts with a God who is intimate, graceful, and persuasive. This starting point, I am convinced, makes all the difference in the world. I wish now to expand on those three qualities of God.

In his own life Jesus experienced God as an intimate presence. Among the number of names for God that were available in his time, Jesus chose "dadda," in his Aramaic language, "Abba." This word begins our revered "Lord's Prayer" as it was gifted to the disciples, that they too might enter this intimacy with God. It would seem that Jesus left the hallowed synagogue and temple, going to the nursery to find the language that expressed his sacred experience.

"Abba-Imma" are among the first words uttered by the newly weaned child, words that reach out for "dadda-mama." I assume that it was this experienced closeness of God in each moment that Jesus offered to us as the genuine relationship with God that might also be ours.

The early church cherished this manner of addressing God and interwove it with many other traditions, some strangely contradictory to the intimacy it represents. Besides being the beginning of the Lord's Prayer, we find "Abba" in two letters of Paul (Galations 4:6; Romans 8:15–16), which is especially telling, since he never knew the human Jesus, only reports of early Christians and the risen Christ. The events reported in which Jesus related to people in a caring and personal mode does seem largely consistent with the claim that he was experiencing God as an intimate, caring presence.

Sadly, not all Christian tradition is graceful; but the parables of Jesus are grace-filled. Parables are unique in that they simply did not exist before Jesus and seldom since Jesus. When we listen to these short, homey stories we are probably as close to the voice of Jesus as we can get. My perspective on forgivness is that God is fully grace and that evidence for this can be found in the words of Jesus. Jesus spoke as Jesus experienced.

The parable of the prodigal is at the top of my list, having made its way into our everyday language as well as classical literature. I expect that only the Good Samaritan is better known, reaching the pinnacle as a name for organizations, hospitals, and buildings. Since the prodigal is well known, let me simply review the essential outline of the story (Luke 15:11–32).

The younger son wants his inheritance now. The father concedes. Although unusual, this act was legal. The son not only squanders his assets, but radically violates his religion in the process. Facing a famine without funds in a foreign land, the son decides to return to be a servant on his father's farm. At least they ate well. He will acknowledge that he has sinned and ask only for refuge in a new status. In fact, the father, with agreement from several elders, could have demanded his son's death for his gross violation of holy law.

Pointedly, the son never had opportunity to utter his request to become a hired servant; rather, the father initiated radical hospitality. The story is told of the parent heaping one gift upon another, not allowing the listener to possibly miss the point that this was a warm and regal welcome. Each gift represents the full reinstatement of the youth as son: running toward him, kissing him, wrapping a robe about him, placing the ring of authority on his finger, fitting the sandals of a free person on his feet, ordering preparations for celebration. No, one could not miss the point. The wandering, squandering youth was met by grace.

While some interpret the parable as one of forgiveness, I prefer to see it as a story of grace, which seems wider and deeper than forgiveness. Of course, the firstborn son is hurt and angered, but even here the parent speaks soothingly to him, "My son, my son." Grace is troubling, to be sure. Often the first sons of the world wish the basic reality to be law and rules, but as I read the parables I hear grace. Persons get what they have not earned!

A second parable makes that graceful point clearly. Each time I have discussed the parable of the vineyard owner (Matthew 20:1–15) with classes, I hear groans of unfairness and claims of not interpreting the story accurately. Society would simply not work on these terms then or today. The story itself is powerful and simple.

A grower wanted to make sure that his crop was harvested in its prime; in this case a vineyard owner was concerned about the grapes. As was customary, early in the morning, the owner went to the town square to hire pickers to harvest. A wage was negotiated for a day's labor. They went to work. Late in the day the owner hired other workers.

Again, according to custom, the workers lined up for their pay at the end of the day. Surprisingly, those who worked only a short time were given a day's wages. Farther back in the line, those who had worked all day, hearing the news, were excited about the larger wage they would receive also.

One of the characteristics of a parable, however, is the unexpected surprise in the story. This is no exception. The daylong workers were given exactly the amount for which they had contracted in the early morning. They were shocked and angry. The owner replied that he had fulfilled his contract with them and asked if they would deny his generosity to others.

The first son grumbled and the daylong workers complained. They accurately saw that fairness not the guideline. They wanted it to be. Grace, however, was the mode. People got what they did not earn. People received gifts.

I find it appropriate to see God in these parables, although the stories are about real people of that era. I interpret the parable as a metaphor for the mode by which God relates to the world. My interpretation is guided by the earlier claim that Jesus was always experiencing the presence of God and would naturally speak from that flow of experience. Jesus, then, saw these events of common people in rural Palestine through the eyes of God. Jesus presented the basic reality of life.

I know that God as fully grace has not been the most popular idea in the history of the Christian church. In fact, Jesus has been called a brief Galilean flicker, his flame nearly extinguished in later eras. We can, however, reach back through all the interwoven strands of tradition and hear the voice of one who experiences an intimate presence and tells stories of grace from those experiences.

It would remain for the twentieth century to understand God

as persuasive. In the systematic cosmology of Alfred North White-
head and its translation into a Christian theology by John B. Cobb,
Jr., the idea of influence takes center stage. It would seem that I am
spanning twenty centuries in my composite picture of God as intimate, graceful, and persuasive; but, in fact, I have relied heavily upon
modern scholarship to make the claims I have about Jesus and his
parables. Also, the vision of a persuasive God has been present in
strands of ancient tradition, not just as a primary and basic quality.

Let us see how persuasion becomes central. The basic reality in
this cosmology is experience, and experience occurs in units termed
occasions. Basic to all creation is the "occasion of experience." Starting
with human experience, the vision spans outward equally toward
the larger and the smaller, the experiences of God and the experiences of animals, plants, cells, molecules, atoms, and subatomic par-
ticles. Such an approach places it clearly in the New Physics and the
post-Modern era. Everything imaginable, all creatures great and small,
is composed of a series of occasions of experience of greater or
lesser complexity.

The occasions of a butterfly are beautiful in themselves but quite
different than those of a lamb, which in turn are quite different from
those of a human person. I think that human experience is as different from God's experience as butterfly experience is of our experience. God is persuasively present in every occasion.

The human moment of experience is the product of several
persuasive events coming together: events in the person's past, events
originating in the person's body, the current complex situations of
the world, and the possibilites offered by God. From the breezes of
these four winds, a person will form who he or she will be in this
moment. Each occasion is of necessity different, having been persuaded by everchanging combinations of multitudes of events. Often we think of our lives as routine, and they are. But no two moments
are exactly alike, if for no other reason than this is the thirty-six-
thousandth time we have put on our seat belt rather than the thirty-
five-thousand-nine-hundred-ninety-ninth time. The familiar habit
is one more experience stronger.

God is ever-present, intimately persuading each and every moment of our experience. As persuader, God is surely the most likely
to know who I will become in my next moment, but even God
does not know until I create myself out of these four ingredients.

This vision surely takes seriously Jesus' experience of God as intimate presence. Echoes of the psalmist resound: Psalm 139–7, "Where can I go from your Spirit?" NRSV. God is within our being, thus could not be any closer. Grace is expressed in offering rich possibilities for persons, but honoring each person's freedom to choose for oneself which possibility to take.

This Christian theology takes another step, expanding the ways in which God is present with persons. Three stand out. God is fully empathic, feeling with us each experience we encounter. Not that God understands only, but that God feels exactly that which we feel, whether it be ecstasy, hurt, passion, sadness, anger, or guilt. From this position of fully knowing us, God then offers a possibility for our next moment that is meant to be healing both for us and all creation. The possibility is realistic and manageable for this person in this context, not "pie in the sky." The possibility, if accepted, will increase our beauty, intensity, love, harmony, and complexity while adding to the common good. God is the persuasive presence who offers us new identity.

A third mode of God's presence is through receiving, holding, and cherishing each of our experiences in God's own life everlastingly. Once an event is completed, we retain it to some degree in our own memory while God is gathering into Godself that same occasion. No event in our lives is ever lost—each and every one is lovingly saved. This conviction is contrary to the familiar saying, "Oh, what difference will it make in a hundred years?" The new answer is that our past events are present to God, cherished and transformed in God's own being.

These three modes of God's being answer our basic human anxiety and despair about being alone, lacking direction, and doubting that our actions matter. God offers, rather, companionship, purpose, and meaning.

Another way of considering God's presence in our lives is to know that God addresses our past, present, and future. God offers us memory of our past that is concluded, yet cherished everlastingly; an awareness of and empathy with those persons and creatures about us right now; and the rich imagination of who we and the creation might become. Persuasively present, speaking to our total being, knowing us through and through, enticing us with who we might become, and lovingly cherishing who we have been, God is with us.

Selecting from important strands of tradition, I have proposed that God is intimate, graceful, and persuasive.

I am fully aware that I have highlighted certain strands of tradition, interpreted those strands, and neglected other strands. I see no way around doing so. One must cut an edge, define a perspective, in order to cast a new light on a perennial and heartbreaking problem. I know that I will differ from other persons, and I am satisfied with that, knowing that I may add to the richness of the conversation occurring about forgiveness.

One cannot bring forward all strands of tradition, for there are profound differences. Reading in scripture that one must forgive seven times seventy (Matthew 18:21) is radically different than another scriptural directive to talk to your offender alone, with another church member, with the entire church, and, if to no avail, treat the offender as a Gentile (vv. 15–17). Translate that, shun them. Seven times seventy, however, sounds like never giving up. When faced with such differences I believe we must be selective and interpretive to locate where we will stand.

Thus, I conclude that the new vision by which I will see forgiveness is that we are blessed with a God who is fully and completely grace. Just as Martin Luther shouted, "Scripture alone," I will proclaim that all we have is grace. Grace is our only guarantee in life. All else is like sand on the beach. Ultimately, I propose, this gracious presence is enough; grace is all that we need. Now I wish to expand more fully the problem of grace versus rights.

Our problem with forgiveness begins with our understanding that we have certain rights, leading us to believe that we deserve something. I hasten to say that I believe in justice, fairness, and rights and have worked diligently for them. I know that often they are present and hold up under duress.

Still, by reading the newspaper and watching TV, we are ripped apart daily by the voices of people for whom those rights have failed. In those lives there comes the natural hurt, rage, and unfairness that accompany that breakdown. Life has not unfolded as they deeply expected it would. The road of life took an unexpected sharp left turn. Bad things have happened to good people.

As an exercise for myself I listed the sources of the guarantees that we expect life to offer us. I began by listing categories: right, commandment, proclamation, declaration, law, code, treaty, vow, oath, pledge, rule, ordinance, standard, contract, convention, warranty, agreement, specification, regulation, principle, duty, honor, value, ethic, moral, trust, obligation, etiquette, fair play, and common courtesy.

From these sources we gain the expectation that we can count on something and that something will be true through thick and thin. We expect that we deserve something.

One of the most powerful statements of rights is found in our American Declaration of Independence: "We hold these truths to be self-evident, that all men [*sic*] are created equal. That they are endowed by their creator with certain inalienable rights and among these rights are life, liberty, and the pursuit of happiness."

Along with this profound statement a number of rights are asserted by which persons order and live their lives: children's rights, animal rights, the right to life, abortion rights, civil rights, voting rights, women's rights, and human rights.

We live by the Ten Commandments, the Golden Rule, the marriage vow, the Pledge of Allegiance, the Universal Code of Military Justice, Hippocratic oath, Robert's Rule of Order, city ordinances, professional standards of practice, state and federal laws, teaching contracts, warranties on automobiles, accepted medical procedures, and the Geneva Convention on treatment of prisoners of war. We live by them expecting justice and fairness, and usually that follows; however, when they break down we are candidates for the process of forgiveness.

As a further exercise, I considered those rights that we often take for granted, then asked if they are ever violated. My findings look frightening:

We affirm the right of a fetus to grow to term and be birthed, but many are interrupted by natural causes or medical procedures. We affirm the right of children to have adequate nutrition, unviolated bodies, clothing, housing, protection from harm; but many are undernourished, suffer abject poverty and are physically and sexually abused. Yes, they surely deserve better, but too often they may not get what they deserve.

Those who labor full time have the right to earn a living wage; for many this is not granted. Women have the right to be treated equally with men, yet the "glass ceiling" is with us, pay inequities still prevail, and the Equal Rights Amendment failed. Employers have a right to expect honesty from employees, yet stealing and embezzling is commonplace. Workers have the right that their pension funds be protected; still, many financial futures have been violated. So, one could add to the list. The point is that every cherished right one can imagine has and is being violated somewhere by someone.

I want to lift up one rather unique right that probably brings forth more disillusionment and rage than any other when violated: the right to be left alone. Other ways of stating it might be the right to live and let live, to be free of interference by another, or to be allowed to mind one's own business. The innocent bystander in the crowd was caught in the hail of crossfire, the knifing victim was standing by the minimart not bothering anyone, the unsuspecting driver was shot as she was legally exiting the freeway. These are often the persons about whom friends say, "But he wouldn't hurt a fly."

These illustrate what we call senseless crimes, totally unprovoked cruelty, random acts of violence. If, however, we consider the interconnection of life, we are brought up short by the realization that as long as anyone anywhere is enraged, despairing, alienated, starving, or distraught, we are all vulnerable and endangered. There is no way for us to stay ultimately aloof, insulated, and separated from the pain and distortion of others. In the drama of life there are no castings held for "innocent bystander"; rather, we all have active intertwining parts.

Our paths intersect in most surprising ways. There appears to be, however, a nearly universal belief in this right to privacy leading to profound devastation when the right is violated. Most of the situations cited in this chapter represent a breakdown in some heartfelt expectation of one right or another.

We live by rights and we live in grace. Rights can fail; grace never fails. We work for rights, we create them, we count on them to live a stable and orderly life, and they are basically good. Grace is not something we work for; rather, it is a gift that we can acknowledge and decide to accept. By living in grace we can increasingly know it to be true in our own experience and can grow to trust in it despite the turbulence of life and the falling away of cherished rights.

The place upon which I stand to view forgiveness is the hill of grace. Again I will note that it is certainly one perspective among many. There are many hills. Others would look from their positions and offer quite different solutions to the persons described here. A starting point for me, then, is that we are in relationship with an intimate, graceful, and persuasive presence. This God offers to us the companionship of understanding and empathy, the security of knowing that direction will come even in the most confusing and baffling moments, and the assurance that what we do in each moment, however insignificant or unknown to others, will be meaningful everlastingly.

Someone knows us and cares for us, wants good things for us, and cherishes what we do. I call this grace. We cannot be ripped away from this intimate relationship; we can leave it, but the relationship will not leave us; we can count on it no matter what life brings. On this we can stand. About this we can have absolute certainty. Nothing else.

I have advocated passionately for my perspective; still, it is this same viewpoint that allows me to enter graciously into dialogue with those of other perspectives. Those perspectives range from the biblical only to the psychological only. We will find no creedal perspectives from the ecumenical councils of our forebears, the Orthodox and Roman Catholic churches. Forgiveness was simply not a fight issue. Passages in the New Testament need to be addressed, especially when they picture God as demanding rather than persuasive.

This dialogue will not occur here, but is postponed for later settings, when I will put on my glasses and invite others to put on their differing glasses to see both the tragedies and the potential solutions. My mode of entering the conversation will be to respect and value their perspectives, exploring where we hold viewpoints in common and where we contrast with one another. I hope that we may ultimately enrich one another such that in the future even more helpful modes of forgiveness will emerge.

The new vision that I am offering here will approach forgiveness in a way that has not been presented before. The understanding of God is so recent that this should be no surprise. The starting point is new. The second newness is that I will affirm a number of paths to forgiveness, not simply one. The basic vision does not change; rather, it allows a variety of streams to bubble forth from the underlying spring. I am hopeful that persons who have thought there was only one way and that way was either unacceptable or impossible for them will find the variety of interweaving paths healing and enlivening. This will be the adventure in which we will engage together.

A third offering is that I will apply this vision of God to a wide range of tragically difficult situations crying out for forgiveness. If the vision is worth its salt, it should speak in a meaningful way to the most tragic of the tragic. I cannot simply choose situations that lend themselves to my vision. Answers must be offered to the good and innocent persons who have been trampled unjustly into the dirt.

Another offering is to consider God's heavenly community. This flight of imagination may well distinguish this vision from others. A continuity will be proposed between the paths of forgiveness during our lifetime and our next adventure beyond our death. I begin with the basic qualities of our relationship with God now and fly toward the imagined relationships at the heavenly banquet in God's community. I affirm that ultimate forgiveness occurs at that table in that community.

A final offering is to close each chapter with a meditation of my own that will offer an affirmation about forgiveness. I do so with the hope that others, reading mine, will revise it so that it may become theirs. Let mine be only the beginning brush strokes on the canvas from which each may paint his or her own picture. This introductory chapter closes with grace.

LIVING WITH GRACE ALONE

Oh, how I long for certainty,
    something I can count on, lean on, stand on.
I need to know what I can do to be safe,
    what will lead me to good things.
I want to awaken to the new day
    with confidence and security.
I desire an anchor, a rock, a foundation,
    a harbor, a lap, a breast, overarching wings.

I plead for guarantees from life,
    asking only that I know my rights.
I do not ask for special rights or favors,
    only for justice.
If I do good,
    I will receive good.
If I treat others kindly,
    they will treat me kindly in return.
If I work hard,
    I will earn the fruits of my labor.
If I am honest with others,
    others will be honest with me.
If I follow the law, code, commandment,
    I will be rewarded accordingly.

I see rights and justice around me,
    hard-won battles of my forbears.
Some of whose names I know,
    others who are remembered only as
    reformers, veterans, abolitionists,
    suffragist, civil rights workers.
Their legacy to me is freedom and opportunity,
    for which I am grateful.

Still, I hear daily of rights violated,
    promises unkept, guarantees unfulfilled,
    treaties broken, trusts shattered.
Some I experience intimately in my own being.
My crying need for certainty, safety, security,
    collide with these many violations.
I question the solidness of the rights about me,
    but I must trust in something,
    or be a ship without a rudder in stormy seas.

I ponder how to achieve certainty.
The universe allows many interpretations of life.
I could obey the divine commandments,
    and look forward to divine justice in the end.

I could affirm the Bible as the inerrant word of God,
    and find within its pages my certainty.
I might follow the natural laws,
    accepting their equally natural consequences.
I could prostrate myself at the church altar,
    and place my faith in traditional doctrine.
I could guide upon the eternal values
    in the classical wisdom of Western culture.
I could turn East, transcending suffering by
    detaching myself from my desires.
I might even give myself to the pragmatic
    and the awesome technology of our day.
Yes, I do know that certainty, rights,
    and guarantees may be sought in many arenas.

I see others seemingly not having such
    strong need for certainty.
I could consider myself one of the lucky,
    seeking solace in life's gated communities.
I could attune myself to body sensations,
    immersing in sensual pleasures.
I might throw myself totally into life as it is,
    creating, discovering, investigating, healing.
I could separate myself from humanity,
    wanting each to tend his or her own garden.
I could constantly foresee and predict,
    allowing my control to be my certainty.

I see even more radical ways of avoiding
    the hurts, injustice, and unfairness of life.
Avoidance looms large as I look about me.
I know that it lives within me as well.
I could keep running so fast I cannot think.
I might become resigned and cynical
    about how little life offers.
I might move into despair and immobilization,
    saying nothing is worth doing.

I could turn from one trivial pursuit to another,
    leaving no energy for anything else.
I could cut out one safe section of reality,
    and call it total reality.
I might numb myself through medication or alcohol,
    distancing the world afar.
But if I am cheated, unrecognized, plagiarized,
    dismissed, downsized, unfaired,
        these avoidant paths are most difficult to walk.

In the crosscurrents of these possibilities
    and my own longing for rights and certainty,
        there comes to me a whisper of another way.
Not a guarantee of all that I deserve,
    or the rights that I might claim,
        or the certainty upon which I may stand.
Rather, a Presence is offered.
Nothing is certain or guaranteed in my life;
    only one guarantee remains;
        nothing can separate me from this Presence.
I am promised steadfast companionship,
    but no map for the journey.
I will know that I am known, fully, totally,
    in all breadth and depth.
I will not know what is ahead,
    only that One accompanies me.

I am promised that this Presence
    desires that I be intense, whole, and beautiful.
I will be offered whispers, calls, and lures
    toward continually new identities.
My life will be a series of becomings,
    each arising from how life unfolds for me.

I am told that I will be cherished now,
    and everlastingly beyond my present life.
Even my worst moments are gathered into
    and held in the loving arms.

But I hear no clarity about the happenings
 of the world or the unfoldings of my life.
So much is left vague, unclear, undefined,
 even dangerous and unsafe.
Living in grace is the response I hear to my
 feverish striving for safety and certainty.
I waiver between trust and mistrust,
 walking with grace and fearfully turning away,
 placing my hand in God's hand and pulling it back.

Can I live this way?
Is grace enough?
I trust it to be so today.
I hope that it will be so tomorrow.

2

But She Broke Her Vow!

Tony was shocked as he looked at the papers he held in his hands. Having just arrived back in town from the restaurant convention, he had greeted his friend Earl, a paralegal in a local attorney's office. It was not the first time he had been served a subpoena regarding his business. However, to read that he had been handed a dissolution of marriage and restraining order from Marcella was beyond belief.

"I can't believe my eyes! Who does she think she is? Why, she's breaking her vow! Don't her promises mean anything?" Tony's dismay quickly moved to blame and anger. He grabbed the phone and punched in his home numbers. Marcella answered. Tony screamed, "Just what do you think you're doing? Is this some kind of sick joke?" All he heard in reply was that his clothes were in the garage and that he had better not talk to her or he would be in contempt of court. Any further talk would have to be with her attorney, another friend of Tony's. She hung up. Tony went reeling and light-headed into the restaurant lounge and poured himself a drink.

Thoughts poured into his mind, things he wished he had said moments before. "You've got it all, girl! Money, a brand new home, a name in this town people would die for, prestige! What do you want? I work my tail off for you and the kids and all you do is complain!"

How Tony would move from his present state of being to forgiveness was to be a long and difficult journey. It is even difficult to know the meaning of forgiveness in this situation, for it does not fit the well-known model. Marcella is not coming on bended knee pleading for his forgiveness. Quite the contrary. She is demanding that Tony stay away from her and having no obvious regrets about their parting. The problem is that if he remains in his present condition he will be filled with negative feelings. He cannot remain there, yet at this moment he has no idea whatsoever about where to go.

There is no question that Tony had his rights violated, that he deserved better than the shock he received.

However, a caring friend does not simply walk over to him, pat him on the back, and say, "You know, Tony, grace is all we've got." Although hopefully Tony will come to the conclusion that life does not always grant what we deserve, that idea is surely a long way in his future. Any true friend must begin where God begins with us, being empathic with where the beloved is at this moment. In Tony's case, to feel with him the dismay, anger, and blame.

If we only look at the moment, taking a cross section of his life, Tony has every right to feel as he does; however, we may need to study history in order to understand the emerging of this painful happening. This moment did not appear out of the blue, but had many events leading to it. Coming to see more fully those events from Marcella's point of view is a significant part of Tony's forgiving her. At this juncture, however, Tony can react only from his shocking wound. Widening his perspective will increase his degree of forgiveness.

Marcella saw marriage as a relationship that, like a garden, needs tending, whereas Tony unknowingly considered her and their marriage more as possessions, things that you have. Once you have found it, you possess it, much like the advertising slogan "A diamond is forever," or like an enduring photo of the smiling and happy bride and groom enclosed in a beautiful frame. Herein lies a basic difference that over their years together led to this tragic moment. We can trace out the story more fully.

Marcella and Tony met at the state college, he majoring in restaurant management, she in nursing. They dated for two years, became engaged, and planned to marry after graduation. Marcella, coming from a family made up of her mother and younger sister, longed for the large, loving family that she had missed due to her father's untimely death. Tony was attracted to the very qualities that lured Marcella to a nursing career—kindness, gentleness, and tenderness. They had spent holidays at each other's homes, and the wider families smiled approvingly upon their love. Shortly after graduation they were married in his home church and she moved with him to his home town.

"Antonio's Restaurant" had been founded by Tony's grandfather. Tony, whose given name was Antonio III, was the third-generation owner. All were proud of him and his friendly, congenial, social qualities that fit him well for his new role. In addition he brought back with him the latest technologies from his college training. Marcella applied early for a position at the community hospital. Both her academic record and the well-known family into which she was marrying helped her to become a nurse in the pediatrics ward.

After two years they agreed it was time to start their family. Tony was well established in the family business, and Marcella had gained enough experience to return part time when the children were older or full time at the time of "empty nest." It seemed to be going well with them. Tony had his caring wife and soon-to-be loving mother to his chidren, and Marcella had that large and well-established family for which she had longed.

The arrival of their second son began an ever-widening separation between them. Tony worked when others played—evenings, holidays, weekends, weddings, anniversaries—the very nature of the restaurant business. Marcella could not count on help with the children, nor times away as a couple. Tears flowed, late night arguments occurred, promises were made and broken.

Between the restaurant and his extended family, Tony was consumed in expectations and obligations, some welcomed, others accepted as duty. He often helped his parents, brothers, or sisters in exactly those tasks that Marcella needed him to accomplish at home. She felt second or third in line for his limited energy. She sat alone on the bleachers at the children's sporting events and school programs. Anger had little impact on his well-defined sense of family duty. From his perspective, he wondered what had become of his tender, loving bride.

Marcella could not have foreseen the implications of moving to

Tony's hometown with a web of relationships already well in place. There were golf games in the summer and racquetball in the winter with his buddies; there was the hostess at the restaurant who was his high school sweetheart. It was not always easy for her to carry out her promise to raise the boys in a church not familiar to her.

Drinks after closing were commonplace, and the evening staff gradually lingered longer. Bitterly, she thought that they had more time with her husband than she did. Thoughts of a possible affair with his former sweetheart frightened her. Marcella wondered many times if her place was to simply complete the picture of the successful man with an attractive wife on his arm followed by their well-behaved and well-dressed children.

She had few true friends, those precious persons who do not come along every day. Yes, she had the sisters, the sister-in-laws, the cousins, the long-term employees. All would warmly greet her, but often Marcella felt it was due to her role as wife to Tony, not because they liked her. Marcella's time working at the hospital was not long enough for her to locate those for whom there was a natural affinity, and clearly not enough time to form bonds. Marcella was lonely. Marcella was largely a single parent. She had few deeper relationships, and she had little time or energy. Nothing she did seemed to reach Tony, let alone persuade him to modify the web in which he was caught.

Tony had reason to wonder where his bride had gone. Marcella did not like the person she was becoming; yet her efforts to transform herself, Tony, or their situation brought her no results. It is no wonder that her recurring dream was being a bird in a gilded cage.

At this moment, however, Tony could see only through the pain of his own wound. She had betrayed him. She had broken trust with him. She had not tried hard enough. She had not given him a chance. She had intentionally hurt him. She had not taken seriously "'til death do us part." Through these lenses Tony saw the situation. His perspective moved him to talk with his own attorney to seek out his rights and to find how he could fight the divorce. He wanted to stop her as well as hurting her just as badly as she had hurt him. He shared his crisis with his family and close friends, seeking their agreement with his justified criticism of her.

In spite of the no-contact order, he scribbled out a hateful letter to Marcella. The flurry of action left him exhausted but still pacing and agitated. The long and short of his activity was that there was little he could do to stop Marcella from her intended plan.

He stopped by his home to pick up his clothes, never seeing Marcella in the process. His sister offered to have him stay in their home until he found his own place. Regular appointments with his attorney, ongoing conversations with family and close friends, and the daily responsibilities of work led Tony into the lonely and bleak routine of life without Marcella.

The mystery of the many unanswered questions hung over him and would not go away. He was a man of divided thoughts at his work, not the usual congenial, social person of the past. He wondered about the "real reason" Marcella was ending their marriage. Tony concluded that there must be another man, someone who took advantage of his long hours away from home. Following out this hunch, Tony drove by the home at various times of day and night, hoping to catch the culprit in the act. He asked friends if they knew of anyone who might be having an affair with Marcella. The results of all his detective work left him with no clues. Perhaps his hunch was wrong.

Tony, like many who have faced an unwanted divorce, could readily be trapped in one of a number of obsessions that would define his truth, give him a purpose, and consume his total energy. Such obsessions are often damaging primarily to the person holding them, but they can just as easily produce violent tragedy to many. Tony might have been stuck in any of the following: "You ruined my life, so I'm going to ruin yours." "If I can't have you, no one else will." "You hurt me, I'm gonna hurt you back real bad." "If I can't trust the one I married, I guess I can't trust anybody." "Marriage just isn't what it's cracked up to be, so you'll never see me walk down the aisle again." "Show me a woman and I'll show you a liar."

Obsessions can be discounts of oneself as well, as the following illustrate: "I took the risk, but never again." "I got left once, so you won't catch me in the position to be rejected again. It just hurt too much." "I guess I'm just not the marrying type." "Maybe there's just something flawed about me."

While Tony would flirt with several of the obsessions, he did not remain imprisoned there. Dismay, anger, and blame lifted slightly to allow the entry of more measured thought about Marcella, himself, and their relationship. Memories crowded in upon his solitary moments; sleep was interrupted and disturbed. The beginning tiny steps of healing were occurring. The obsession with his own wound was giving way slightly to other understandings.

Tony's situation is one of a class of offenses that occur to us. His is only one illustration that points toward many other betrayals life can offer us, although it is particularly poignant because in marriage we are so fully intertwined and so completely vulnerable. I have chosen this situation just because it is one of the most devastating losses we face. All facets of a person are present and revealed in a marriage, making the depth of hurt potentially the deepest. Nevertheless, it is like any number of broken promises in a variety of settings. Rights that are thought to be guaranteed disappear; benefits that are thought to be deserved vanish.

In some manner someone breaks trust with another. The event may be minor, such as not keeping the lunch date with a friend, forgetting to pick up one's spouse from a doctor's appointment, or not remembering a birthday. Other events may be of severe, even deadly, consequences, such as secretly spending the money that was set aside to pay taxes, running up the debt on credit cards so as to require bankruptcy, or infecting one's spouse with HIV after a clandestine affair.

A brother may take advantage of both parents and siblings by continually borrowing from the older generation's limited income; a business partner may leave the firm taking a majority of clients; a long-term accountant may have secretly embezzled over a number of years; a close friend may have told others information that a person shared in strictest confidence.

The present story addresses these types of events.

For one seeking guidance on how to forgive, it may be necessary to translate this illustration from the realm of marriage to the offense that fits one's condition more fully. Now, on with the story.

The first time Tony saw Marcella after he was served the legal papers was at their initial settlement hearing with their attorneys. Since there seemed to be civil talk between them in that controlled setting, Marcella called him the next day and asked that they meet privately. Tony did not yet know that she had lifted the restraining order immediately after the hearing. They met in a quiet restaurant on the outskirts of town. Though painful, here began the dawning of a wider perspective on Marcella and the divorce proceedings.

Naturally, Tony attempted to persuade Marcella to stop the process and let them try again. She had shaken him from his complacency and now he was awake. Her shock treatment had worked. He knew that he needed to change his ways. He spoke of the new resolutions he would carry out for her and the boys. Marcella listened and shook her head. She had watched him carefully over the years, identifying his natural way of living and his priorities. She had gathered enough data from the experiment of their marriage. She asked rather for a cordial relationship between them and a partnership regarding their common interest in their boys.

Seeing that his initial request was rebuffed, Tony spoke of his anger and disappointment in her breaking their vows. He questioned her honesty and her ability to stick it out through thick and thin. Had she really taken marriage seriously? Did she really comprehend that she spoke that oath in the presence of God? Was nothing sacred to her? Didn't any of the ceremony mean anything to her? His forceful words, like those of the Grand Inquisitor, ripped Marcella where she was most vulnerable. Tears flowed; she looked away, then started to leave but remained with the promise that Tony would listen to her side of the story.

Marcella began her own story of betrayal. Her need for a large, loving family had turned into a lonely desert. Her deepest desire to be central in the life of her husband was reduced to sharing this space with his parents, brothers, sisters, and long-term friends. Her need for an intimate and sharing companionship had become living with the leftovers of Tony's energy and time. Her dream of shared parenting with their boys became a nightmare of handling it all herself. Her anticipation of being active in the community translated into being on call for command performances with Tony.

Tony began to understand that he was not the only one who was betrayed, only the most recent one. He began to see the fullness of the present situation, that each of them had losses, not merely that he had been wounded. Sadness and regret accompanied him as he drove away from that meeting. If only he had known in those many past moments what he knew today. "Why didn't I see it?" And now his beloved was saying that it was too late. The blame that he had put upon Marcella earlier had now circled around and was pointed at himself.

This increasing self-blame over the next several weeks pushed Tony to call for another meeting. He had painfully sifted through the events and feelings that Marcella had shared. He began to see her in a new light, not the clouded vision of his own pain and anger. However, a new issue arose from this unwelcome reminiscing: "Why hadn't Marcella told him sooner?" Yes, he now began to get the picture, but it was too late. He placed this question before her. Both knew that just beneath it lay a reservoir of anger and blame toward her. He was convinced that if he had known earlier, he could have fixed it.

"I told you a hundred times in a hundred ways! You just would not hear me. You were too involved in your world!" Now Tony was completely confused. "When and where did you tell me?" In an exasperated voice, Marcella tried the one-hundred-and-first time. The fact that Tony had never heard her clearly was the very reason that Marcella saw no hope and took the unilateral action in filing for divorce. Unknowingly, Tony had supported her case.

Marcella recounted the many times: when she was ill that night late in their first pregnancy, but he had to work an important party; when she wanted to leave for a weekend together, but Tony had made plans for them with his couple friends; when he had left to put in a sink in his parent's kitchen when their own garage was in dire need of cleaning; when they had planned for a romantic evening after his night shift ended, but he stayed to socialize with coworkers at the restaurant; when their eldest son was playing his champion-ship midget league game, but he called at the last minute due to the unexpected arrival in town of a sales representative.

Had he not felt her unhappiness? Had he not seen her tears? Had he not read her body language of withdrawal? Had he not heard her words of anger, gradually growing to be cynical and re-signed? Did she need to swing the proverbial "two-by-four" to cap-ture his attention? That Marcella could not seem to get his attention brought her the most hopeless feelings. How could she be impor-tant to him if it required such a production for him to listen to her?

These words hit Tony below the belt, for they questioned his sense of loyalty and duty to his wider family, his own family, and his career. Indeed, he felt his manner of loving was beinq questioned. Was not his devotion to work a way of loving his own family? Did not his faith and his family heritage guide him to care for many people, to keep the web open and ever expanding? Could not Marcella see that he was a giving person and cooperate with him, not fight him? She might, in fact, have been the more selfish of the two, wanting so much of his attention and time. He had fully hoped that she would encourage his many relationships and activities.

This conversation ended on a sour note. Both were required to weigh the viewpoint expressed by the other. Their cluster of needs and constellation of values exhibited some profound differences. Their differences were basic. The meetings had brought them to more understanding of each other and the significant moments of their shared relationship.

One serious question remained in Tony's mind. In their next meeting he posed it to her. "Marcella, now honestly, did you try hard enough?" Expecting the question, Marcella answered a firm, "Yes! You cannot possibly know the number of times I awoke in the morning vowing to myself that today I would be happy and do all I could to make you happy. The problem is that by midmorning I had broken my own promise to myself. I tried hard. I tried for a long time. I kept failing myself. I couldn't do it. I simply gave up."

Tony knew Marcella's determination well enough to realize that she spoke the truth. He need not question her any more. Had he been able to listen better, they might have tried together before she reached the point of no return. He realized that he was accountable for his lack of listening.

In his own reflection Tony came to understand more about who Marcella was then and is now. She had a different understanding of love, of marriage, of loyalty. Likewise, Tony knew that in their basic orientation to life he was cut from a different fabric. Those things most natural to him, as well as satisfying to him, caused Marcella the greatest grief and consternation. Perhaps he need not blame her or blame himself.

He concluded that Marcella needed an attentive companion who made their relationship central in his life, while Tony knew himself to be one who had a host of relationships of great importance to him. The slogan "All I need are a few close friends" would not fit him. The listening that Marcella wanted was that of primary dedication to that relationship. Tony listened as one with many important relationships.

Tony emerged from a number of meetings with Marcella with a widely expanded perspective. Beginning with the primary feelings of anger and blame and defining himself as the injured party, he gradually moved to a person who better understood his own complexity, Marcella's complexity, and how these complexities intermixed in the history of their relationship. He understood that they would probably never be satisfied nor bring satisfaction to one another.

Widening his perspective allowed him to increase his awareness of the present and the possible futures. Saved from his immersion in hurt, anger, and blame he was freed to work with Marcella on a parenting plan for the boys, seeking their well-being under these new circumstances. Financial settlements could be focused upon that which would allow both parties to grow and blossom from this point forward.

It was also necessary for them to grieve the future by accepting the loss of all their hopes and dreams. Such is never an easy or quick process and often makes up a significant part of the grief of the forgiving process. Each stood before the altar with anticipation and hoped that in the state of matrimony their basic needs would be met. Instead, dreams were shattered by the reality of the relationship.

For Tony the primary loss was that of his small family within his larger family and hometown community. Significant strands in his web of life were now missing. Marcella questioned whether her need for an intimate relationship could be met. She knew that it had not happened with Tony. The question remained open as to whether it would be possible with another. Only the future would tell her the degree of her loss. In the meantime she would nurse parttime at the hospital and be the best mother she could when the boys were with her. A limited relationship between Tony and Marcella was all that seemed possible for the immediate future.

I have focused upon the journey of Tony, as he is the primary subject of our story. Marcella had her own process of forgiveness to go through, and that would require another story. Tony may be likened to Dante walking through the depths of Hell with his guide Virgil, although most of the time he was not aware of the Gracious Companion whispering in the bleakest hours of possible tiny steps forward and of glimmers of hope ahead. His was not a single path like Dante's, for many times he would be hurled back to "square one" again with wrenching pain, anger, and vengeance. Each repetition, however, became shorter, with less time spent in the unbearable feelings.

This gracious whispering prompted moving from seeing everything through the pain of his own wound to seeing Marcella as the complex person she is. Perception expanded. A divine persuasion calls all of us toward empathy with increasing areas of the creation, to love what God loves. Deepening empathy and widening perception were the paths Tony walked.

That Tony was aware of and accepting of more facets of his own being were important, just as was his expanding understanding of Marcella. More important was that he not be trapped in one of several obsessions such that he would not be open to the possibility of new modes of being for himself, for Marcella, and for their relationship. To be imprisoned by hurt, anger, blame would squeeze the life from him, for he would have neither time nor energy to listen to the divine persuasions in his life. The journey leading to deeper, richer life would be blocked. This pathway to forgiveness offers not only inner peace but also openness to the dynamic transformations that can come from the Gracious One.

SEEING THE OTHER IN A NEW LIGHT

I hurt.
The pain won't let go.
I see red.
Something in me is destroyed.
I cannot stop these feelings.
You hurt me.
I blame you for what I feel.
I want to hurt you back.
I am consumed.
I want justice.

I want someone in a black robe to
    make you suffer.
I want you to hurt as I do.
If only I could blank it all out,
    but try as I may, only temporary relief comes.
I go in a circle.
I hurt, I hate, I blame.
I am stuck and cannot break free.
But I know there is more to me
    than these circling feelings.
I long to get back my old self.
Perhaps my knowing will help me.
I can remember being happy and productive,
    when life tasted good.
I know that now I have a deep wound.
I will never be the same again.
But I hope for more than being wounded.
Might I be an observer looking in on me?
Could I see better?
I could see both my feeling and my thinking.
This allows me to see more of me.
Yes, I can still think
    when I am not seeing red.
I am more than my feelings.
But I do not want to deny my precious feelings.
I dash back and forth between
    feelings and knowing.
Perhaps for brief moments I might
    be able to be aware and think.
I know that You are gracious
    and also grace the one who wounded me.
How much I wish that You didn't!
I want You to join me in blame,
    telling me that I am right in doing so.
I want You to comfort me by
    reassuring me that the other
    will be shunned by You.
Could You not punish the other

right away or at least later on?
I can only address You for a short time,
    then must rush back to my feelings.
Another day I return to You,
    pleading that You side with me.
However, my awareness will not allow me to
    ask You to be who You are not.
It troubles me that You lure me to
    love what You love.
For to do so means an unbelievable
    stretching to see the other
    through Your eyes.
I rush back once again to my circle
    of hurt, hate, blame,
    and momentarily feel better.
I loathe the one whom You grace.
We are not in the same sphere.
But You grace me as I run my circle.
I know You feel whatever I feel
    and want the best for me.
I want to block out that You
    are continually wishing
    the best for the other.
I resist that You graciously
    love the other.
There must be more to the other
    than what I see.
If You spend Your time with this
    one who hurt me, I wonder
    what You see.
I do not want to admit it,
    but if there is more to me than wound
    there must be more
    to the other than the wounder.
Surely Your divine eyes see more in
    both of us than I can see.
You must feel more with both of us
    than that I am consumed by my wound

and that the other relishes wounding others.
I know that You continually whisper to me.
Yet my pain blocks out Your voice;
      when seeing red I cannot hear.
When have I ever needed Your nearness
      and Your touch more than now?
I need to be in touch with You,
      listening for Your desires for me,
      new identities You wish for me.
I do know I thrive by Your grace,
      not just my own doing.
Perhaps I can live in the tension of
      feeling my own pain,
      accepting this wound,
      listening to Your whispers,
      knowing that You grace me,
      knowing that You grace the other,
      searching for a greater fullness
      of both myself and the other
      and sensing Your grace
      encircling us both.

3

I'm Still All Black-and-Blue

Rosa awoke in pain. Her left shoulder throbbed and she could not open one eye. She could hear the children playing in the living room and was glad that Juan was not there. He would be home soon after finishing his graveyard shift at the Alcoa plant. She changed positions several times to see if she would feel better. Looking toward the window, she tried to bring things into focus with her right eye; everything seemed blurry. Nothing seemed to help her feel better, and she knew that the children needed breakfast prepared and lunches packed before school. She took a deep breath and slowly found her footing on the floor.

She made her way to the bathroom, dreading to look in the mirror. Grimmacing, she gently washed her face and saw the eye swollen and stuck shut, surrounded by skin colored black-and-blue. A dreaded but familiar sight was before her. She wondered at the number of times she had been through this morning ritual. Most of all, she knew that she had better get on the move to get the children ready for school, or there might be even more trouble. As she opened the bedroom door she braced herself for the blaring television and the barrage of questions from her three children.

In that short lull between children running for the bus and Juan returning from work, Rosa turned off the television and flopped down in the easy chair. These were some of her most precious moments, times of peace and quiet. But today her pain interrupted her quietness and brought her back to the night before. She tried to remember what had started it all. It was probably some silly argument about one of their children. At least, that's how it usually began. She knew that it didn't take much. She feared any small argument, for she had learned where they would go all too quickly.

Rosa remembered. It was Manuel's basketball shoes. She had gone with him to pick them out, and he would have nothing but the latest Michael Jordan brand. At dinner when Manuel had shown them proudly to his father, a volcano erupted. Naturally the blame went to Rosa. He thought that she had more sense than to pay that much for a growing boy's feet. He would need a new pair in three months. Then came the speech on money, that old familiar lecture. When Rosa said they could talk about it later, not during dinner, Juan pushed her, chair and all, to the floor.

Something snapped in Rosa. She burst into loud screaming and could not stop. She was running for the door, screaming as she went, when Juan grabbed her, hit her in the face, knocking her to the sofa. Before she could make a move he covered her mouth with his hand as he yelled for her to be quiet. Rosa went limp, utterly defeated again. Deep sobs rose from her gut, hot tears mixed with the blood from her eye. Manuel and Juanita ran to her aid, but Juan yelled at them to go back to the table and finish their dinner. Soon Rosa's deep sobs faded into rhythmic whimpers, then silence. This same silence pervaded all who remained at the table.

The old familiar hopelessness engulfed Rosa as she sat staring into space, totally unaware of her surroundings. Increasingly she lived in this helpless and hopeless sphere. She was dumbfounded about her screaming. It was new. She didn't know what had come over her, since all the other times when he hurt her, she had simply taken it in silence, hoping that this would cause him to stop sooner. There had been many years of violence, beginning soon after their marriage. Even during their dating, Rosa had been able to see it for what it was. She puzzled over this new development in their relationship: screaming!

Rosa moved slowly to the medicine cabinet, shook out several of her prescribed pain pills, and wished she had something stronger that would simply end it all. It would be so easy to go to sleep and not wake up. This familiar wish passed away as she walked to the shelf in the pantry, reached for the bottle of wine hidden in the back, poured a large glass, then sat again in her comfortable chair. She hoped for the usual, that the pills would reduce her pain and the wine would numb her mind. Many times it was better for her to just not think.

She could not, however, quell the question of whether this time she could heal without seeing her physician. She was running low on excuses about how each accident occurred, especially when she knew that her doctor was already growing increasingly suspicious. She would not think about it, and hope for the best. Just then she remembered the Tuesday women's luncheon and felt another loss. She could not go looking this way. There would be too many embarrassing questions or more polite, questioning stares. She just knew that shame would engulf her. Others would know that things were not going well, life was not working for Rosa. Another excuse was needed. Her isolation reached a new high.

This could at least be a peaceful moment in her swirling, chaotic life. She would not even allow herself to think about the number of pills and glasses of wine it was now requiring for her to gain entry to her quiet place.

Rosa was awakened by Juan's voice. She had drifted off to sleep and not heard his pickup enter the driveway or him coming into the house. His cheery voice gave her the clear impression that the other Juan was now present. He greeted her and touched her on the shoulder, speaking of what had happened during his shift that night, while acting as though nothing had happened at dinner. Rosa had little to say. She was sleepy, numbed, and cautious. Only his need for breakfast stirred her from the chair.

As they sat during breakfast, Juan told Rosa to put something on her eye. She replied that she didn't yet know what to do about it. This led him to tell her in a calm, persuasive voice that she had to stop provoking him. She had made him do it, even though he had not wanted to hurt her. There was nothing else he could have done. He honestly did not like their fighting any more than she did.

But she certainly should know that they did not want the neighbors to hear their family squabbling. After all, they had only been living in this new neighborhood several years. Juan knew that he would not punish her if only she would use common sense and make the right decisions. She should know what they could afford on his salary, and she had to learn to tell Manuel that he couldn't have everything television told him he couldn't live without.

She was to be the boss, not the children. He knew that they respected him and wouldn't try some of the tactics they used on her. "Once you draw the line and they know you mean it, they will stop pushing you around." Rosa listened quietly, for this, too, was a familiar lecture in their cycle of abuse. Though he did not know, she knew of the three children's fear of Juan. He called it respect, but she had listened to their distress too often. The feeling was called fear.

Rosa was relieved when Juan got up from the table and went to bed. She wondered which actions disgusted her the most, the hitting or the syrupy-sweet, self-righteous lectures. She searched out some ointment for her eye, carefully washing the bruised area, while wondering how long she would have to stay home to avoid the embarrassment of others' staring at her. Quietly, so as not to disturb Juan's sleep, Rosa went about tidying up the house. As she did so, she was not aware that she was dying a slow, tedious spiritual death, her life sapped out of her by each act of violence and by each lecture about her weakness and failures.

Three years before, Rosa had reached a breaking point and sought out the pastor of a nearby neighborhood church. She poured out her story of stress, anger, hitting, making up, and starting once again with tension rising. The pastor was the first person to be trusted with the inner life of this supposedly happy family, a risk weighed by Rosa for months before she acted. She needed to know what was right in the view of God and how to carry out that right behavior. Although Rosa was not active in any church, she had many perfect attendance pins from church school in her childhood and even today continued an active life of daily prayer.

Pastor Martinez listened attentively with a caring attitude. She shared her dilemma of finding their present life unbearable, yet knowing that God wanted her to stay in her marriage and give their children a good home. The pastor agreed with her on what God wanted. He opened his Bible and pointed out the requirements of forgiving offenses seventy-times-seven times, of accepting any apology Juan made and reconciling with him, and of being submisive to her husband just as the Church is to Christ. She had received her answer.

The pastor prayed with her, asking God to forgive Rosa for her rebelliousness and Juan for his angry violence. He asked that the Holy Spirit enter their marriage and bring repentance to both Rosa and Juan, leading them to a new depth of love. Concluding their time together, he offered to meet with Rosa and Juan together to look at the scriptural basis for their marriage and the role of husband and wife. While Rosa thanked him for that opportunity, she knew full well that she could not invite Juan. She had not even told him she was talking to the pastor, fearing he would block even that first step. How could she possibly tell him about the meeting that the pastor wanted to hold with them? Sadly she walked away from the church, feeling that her own sense of failure had been accurate and that God was displeased with who she had been. The path of righteousness ahead seemed that much more impossible to walk. Her head swirled with the words she had just heard: seventy times seven...failure... apology...repentance...submission...! Deep shame surrounded and encased each word. Rosa would, however, try across the next several years to follow the Bible.

Temptations abounded for her during those years. Thoughts that would not go away lured her from doing the right thing. The rifle was the most agonizing. When Juan was sleeping, after she had awakened in pain once again, the urge to load a round, sight in on the sleeping form, and pull the triggger was compelling. More often she pictured the seldom-used suitcase high on the closet shelf. She could simply disappear one day. Nevertheless, the idea that won most often was the wine bottle, carefullly hidden and secretly re-plenished.

Other solutions brought with them so much damaging harm to family. She would suffer, not make others suffer. Her great love and loyalty to her children would not let her leave by disappearing, going to prison, or snuffing out her own life. She continued on her chosen pathway, enjoying the few pleasures that came along and accepting the increased price the alcohol was costing to her own health. Ideas can imprison, and ideas can liberate. For Rosa, the beliefs she held vaguely, which were confirmed by the pastor, entrapped her in a life that could not be sustained.

Rosa represents a number of women caught in the web of domestic violence. Trapped by intimidation from the person she chose to marry, the vows she made at the altar, the growing needs of her children, the financial pressures of home mortgage and car payments, and the shame of failing in her most important dream, she is rendered immobile. Adding to the intensity of this imprisonment is her religious belief that she must continually accept an apology, forgive, and try again. Abuse of the elderly and the developmentally challenged are variations on this theme, although the nature of their insurmountable walls may be different. Rosa's story is an effort to present forgiveness as a new door for her escape!

Then came Maria. She was a long-term friend who lived nearby. On this day, Maria would not walk away when Rosa did not answer her soft calling at the door. Rightly, she sensed that this was another one of those morning-after events for Rosa. Finally the door opened a crack, revealing only one side of Rosa's face. Maria knew that he had done it again. She barged in!

The conversation that ensued between them proceeded like this:

"Rosa, you can't let him go on doing this to you!"
"That's easy for you to say. You have a good man."
"Thats's not the point, Rosa."
"So what am I supposed to do?"
"Well, something different than this!"
"I have to think of the kids."
"Of course, that's why you've gotta do something."
"So shall I shoot him, me, or disappear?"
"Honey, there has to be a better way."
"Wish I could think of one."
"I just know you can."
"I have to live with myself, you know."
"That's right, you do."
"The Bible says I have to keep forgiving him."
"Really?"
"Yes, and I'm supposed to submit to him."
"Wow!"
"That's what being a wife is all about."

"Not very appealing, to be sure."

"Well, at least I know I'm pleasing God."

"That sure is important."

"I can suffer if I know it's right in God's eyes."

"You sure have done a lot of suffering."

"I cannot be disloyal to God."

"And you think God wants you to go through this?"

"That's what the pastor said."

"You heard that from a pastor?"

"Yes, about three years ago; I talked with him."

"I never knew you had done that."

"He showed me right in the Bible what to do."

"You mean forgive, make up, and submit."

"That's what it said as plain as day."

"Rosa, it must say something else, too."

"Like what do you mean?"

"Like God loving us more than the sparrow."

"No, he didn't show me that."

"How about, 'Come unto me all ye who labor.'"

"He just pointed to the other ones."

"Did he talk about the bad boy, the prodigal?"

"No."

"There's just more to the Bible than he said."

"Really? Like another side to the story?"

"Absolutely. It's more like a love story anyway."

"But what about my part, my duty?"

"I guess it's mainly to know that you're loved."

"OK, but what about the have-to's?"

"I think it's more like getting a wonderful gift."

"I'm afraid you're muddying the water for me."

"Dear friend, we need to talk a lot more."

"Why not? It couldn't be worse than this."

Thus began a number of conversations over the next several months. The two major questions in their talks were, "Must I forgive?" and "Does forgiveness mean reconciliation?" Even to raise the questions empowered Rosa, for they engaged her thinking about a possible doorway besides those destructive portals she had been contemplating for years. She might be able to be on good terms with God and not have to endure the continuing abuse. That new idea spelled freedom to Rosa. The imprisonment by ideas might end.

After a particularly violent beating and several days in the hospital, Rosa gathered the children and escaped to a safe home. While they were there it was arranged that Rosa would offer child care to a family that would provide her and the children with a place to live over the summer. During this time she would reflect on what to do next. She wanted most of all to make an informed decision, not one impulsively made in the midst of a fiery moment. Staying safe by not letting Juan know where she was and choosing when to telephone him would help her know the next step.

It was no suprise to Rosa that her first call home elicited rage from Juan. He was filled with anger and humiliation. Rosa simply hung up. Later conversations found the anger fading as Juan brought out the familiar apology while pleading with her to come home. Later he even promised to seek out a professional and work on his problem of anger. He was convinced that they would have to do this together, and to give it any chance of working at all they had to live under the same roof. Rosa held steady, having heard all these promises and good intentions before. She suggested Juan start on his own, working out his issues while she considered whether she would join him.

Our story concludes with Rosa pondering her profound decision. Whether conditions will be such that a sustainable reconciliation between Rosa and Juan is possible remains to be seen. The separation might, on the other hand, be the first step toward ending their relationship. So much depends upon Juan and his willingness to enter a program of change, in radical contrast to his easily crafted apology. Rosa will need continual replenishing of her newly found belief that God does not wish her to suffer needlessly. In fact, the battered women of the world come to differing conclusions about the next step in an abusive relationship.

The story allows us to focus on several primary issues regarding forgiveness: Must we forgive? Is reconciliation the only form of forgiveness? May self-protection be an important part of the process of forgiveness? The second issue has already been addressed in our first story of Tony and Marcella. I answer the first two questions "No," while to the third I respond "Yes." Now we enter a more careful consideration of how I come to the answers I have offered.

Pastor Martinez is right. The Bible does say that you must forgive. Maria is right also, that the Bible says much more than that. I wish to examine more closely the passages to which the pastor pointed. Peter approaches Jesus with the question: "Lord, if another member of the church sins against me, how often should I tell you, I forgive? As many as seven times?" Jesus said to him, "Not I tell you, seven times, but seventy times seven." (Matthew 18:21–22). Luke frames a similar saying in the context of Jesus speaking to the disciples: NRSV: "Be on your guard! If another disciple sins, you must rebuke the offender, and if there is repentance, you must forgive. And if the same person sins against you seven times a day, and turns back to you seven times and says, 'I repent' you must forgive." (Luke 17:3–4).

These passages leave no doubt that persons are to embody a forgiving way of life. Rather than take the numbers literally, for we see evidence of the mystical number seven, it seems more appropriate to assume that the meaning is to forgive without ceasing. Only one of the two passages notes repentance as a stage in the forgiving process.

The Lord's Prayer, probably the most frequently uttered words in the Christian church, is often quoted as making forgiveness mandatory. Matthew records the second petition of the prayer: "And forgive us our debts, as we also have forgiven our debtors..." (Matthew 6:12). Luke's version is: "and forgive us our sins, for we ourselves forgive everyone is indebted to us" (Luke 11:4). Clearly there is a reciprocal relationship between our request for forgiveness and our granting forgiveness to others. The prayer assumes that the petitioner is now forgiving or has already forgiven other persons. We might have some reservations about forgiveness that are motivated by a requirement. Whether simply assumed or radically required, again the process of a forgiving lifestyle is held before us.

Matthew, in his commentary following the prayer, highlights the requirement side of the argument: "For if you forgive others their trespasses, your heavenly Father also will forgive you; but if you do not forgive others, neither will your Father forgive your trespasses." (Matthew 6:14–15). Mark joins the chorus on this theme: "Whenever you stand praying, forgive, if you have anything against anyone; so that your Father in heaven may also forgive you your trespasses." (Mark 11:25) Even more powerful is an additional verse added by other ancient authorities: "But if you do not forgive, neither will your Father who is in heaven forgive your trespasses." Nothing is left unclear in these three passages. Forgiveness is necessary to gain forgiveness.

A most striking passage to speak of the requirement of forgiveness is the commentary on the parable of the unforgiving servant. The story reports that after being forgiven a massive debt, the servant imprisons a debtor who owes him a pittance. In the final moments of the story the forgiving king, hearing of this action, recalls his servant…"And in anger his lord handed him over to be tortured until he would pay his entire debt." The commentary on the story adds: "So my heavenly Father will also do to every one of you, if you do not forgive your brother or sister from your heart" (Matthew 18:34–35).

This commentary is vividly clear in its belief that forgiveness is a necessary condition to be forgiven. Jesus' sermon on the plain scores a similar point: "Forgive, and you will be forgiven;…for the measure you give will be the measure you get back." (Luke 6:37–38).

It is possible, then, to conclude from these passages that our being forgiven is conditioned by whether or not we forgive others. If we do, we are forgiven by God; if we do not, we are not forgiven by God. We determine by our own actions whether we will warrant forgiveness. We make our own beds and must then sleep in them. If such is true, and if forgiveness means reconciliation without protection, then Rosa was led astray by Maria, and she would have been better off spiritually to endure her suffering.

A slightly different voice is also heard from scripture. Three steps are provided for a person who has been sinned against by a "brother": privately go and tell him of his fault, speak again in the presence of one or two others, and share your grievance with him in the gathering of the church. If in each of these stages you are not heard, then "let such a one be to you as a Gentile and a tax collector" (Matthew 18:15–17). The sinner is shunned and reviled, like those outside the pale of God's love and the traitors to God's people. The implication is clear that forgiveness has its limits. Contrary to seventy times seven or seven times a day, we hear you may change your forgiving stance to one of derision if the proper steps have been followed. We could seriously question to what degree such steps would have helped Rosa, since she would not have dared to speak to Juan in those terms, to say nothing of trying to get him to the pastor or a church service.

Apart from its helpfulness to Rosa, all this is to say that the Bible does not offer a monolithic statement about forgiveness; rather, there are strands of contrasting traditions side by side. There are also differing methods of interpreting those varied traditions. One method is that of affirming the Bible to be the inerrant word of God, verbally dictated to the authors. For such believers the quoted passages make the case and prove the point that forgiveness is mandatory to receive God's forgiveness. The apparent inconsistencies would be considered mysteries yet to be understood, but not to call into question their truth and authority.

I am not a fundamentalist Christian, so I do not follow that line of reasoning. Rather, I am a progressive Christian, meaning that I am an interpreter of scripture. In this sense, I will follow Maria's lead when she says that the Bible says more than those verses quoted by Pastor Martinez. I think that we are closest to the authentic words of Jesus when we are hearing the parables. Allow me to explore their relevance to forgiveness.

It is intriguing to me that the wayward son, when returning to his father's farm, never has opportunity to give voice to the price he should pay for his sin, to be treated not as a son, but as a hired servant (Luke 15:21). The father's graceful welcome occurred before the son had a chance to blurt out his rehearsed words. I see no requirement in this transaction. The father sees the son at a distance walking toward home; the father responds.

The vineyard owner initiates offering a day's pay for those workers who had labored only an hour (Matthew 20:9). Clearly there was no requirement met by the workers; rather, the gift was offered unconditionally.

Even the parable of the unforgiving servant may have gained its usual interpretation through the final verse that is not a part of the story but an added commentary to the story (Matthew 18:35). Much as Aesop's fables always end with a moral, so this parable concluded with a teaching, a practice that is not characteristic of Jesus. More likely we have here an addition by the gospel writer speaking for a community who proclaimed Jesus as Christ, rather than Jesus who originally was proclaimer. Hearing the story without the final verse leads me, rather, to interpret that none of the servants truly understood the generosity of the king; thus all stood in need of transformation.

We are called in our review of scripture to weigh whether forgiveness is grounded in requirement or generosity, for both are present. It is obvious that I advocate generosity. Rosa heard contrasting views from Pastor Martinez and Maria, representing those differences expressed by interpreters of scripture. We might summarize that in scripture forgiveness is held in great esteem by all as something that is good and appropriate to do, whereas some elevate it to the level of requirement.

While we have spent much time discussing the Bible, as a person immersed in the Wesleyan tradition, I must also search out other sources of wisdom besides scripture. Here I affirm four sources of authority: scripture, tradition, reason, and experience. I place none in priority, but rather believe that power lies in their merging and blending so as to enrich one another.

For this reason I now turn to a vision of God, to theology. A God who exacts requirements and a God of total grace meet like a discordant, screeching collision. I have proclaimed a God of intimacy, persuasion, and grace. There is simply an inconsistency between those qualities and a God who would say that we must do something. Total grace does not demand! In the basic unit of experience, the human occasion, God whispers of new possibilities in the midst of all the other powerful persuaders in our lives. The final decision lies with the person, a conclusion forged of the many persuasive "what is's" and the one "what might be" from God.

I invite you to join me for a few moments as we take a guided tour of the tiny occasion of experience where human and divine meet. We see several important features of this awesome event. First, God is always present, like a faithful committee member never missing a meeting. Nothing that we can do would keep God out of this crucible of creative energy. If we thought of colors, the red of God would always be in the picture to some degree. Second, the other persuasive events wax and wane in their presence, some more active in the waking state, others in dire pain, still others in a deafening tornado. At times their colors would be barely perceptible. All blend and merge, as on an artist's palette, their persuasive powers creating the next moment. The picture painted in the previous moment highly influences the next picture, but in a series of occasions the subject changes dramatically, as if reds, oranges, and yellows shift to blues, grays, and blacks.

If that is true, and I believe it to be so, then how is it that God would not forgive us? No matter what we do, God will be present, offering us some manner of possibility. God does not leave. God is always present. Admittedly, the nature of God's next lure must be in some measure in tune with the last happening, but that is only to say that the new possibility must be relevant and manageable. This picture of God's manner of relating to the world and the concept that God will not forgive us are not compatible. They are in different worldviews, and essentially that is my point. My vision of God does not allow for God to not forgive.

Returning to Rosa, I wonder at the thousands upon thousands of possibilities from God that Rosa become someone more than she was in her moments of distress. There were the tiny whispers, barely audible, to seek the wisdom of a pastor, to allow Maria to go through the door, and to gather the children and leave. All must have been offered many times and been rejected as too frightening before on one particular day they were finally grasped. The few peaceful moments Rosa experienced in her chair must have been fostered and enhanced by God's offering of peace.

The depth of empathy shown by God during brutal violence, excruciating pain, peaceful aloneness, utter hopelessness, and reconciling pleasure, must have provided the grounding from which God created and offered realistic possibilities to Rosa.

I want to distinguish between God's desiring that we forgive and demanding that we forgive. The first I affirm; the latter I reject. God does will, I believe, that we live in harmony in all relationships: human, animal, plant, inorganic, global, and universal. God's desire for grace and beauty prompts this harmony. When Rosa, like so many others, is consumed with physical pain, traumatic fear, abject unworthiness, violent impulses, and overwhelmed helplessness, she is simply unavailable to be transformed into the person she might be if she were able to listen to both her own intuition and God's luring.

To forgive is to set the stage for transforming possibilities that bring pleasure to Rosa, the creation, and God. No one could possibly wish more for Rosa to live in mutually forgiving relationships than God, yet realistically she remained captured at some distance from that realm. As she lives in protection, however, there will be increased opportunity for her to blossom into one of the many beautiful flowers that God yearns for her to become.

What I have to offer to Rosa is the conviction that strands of scripture and a vision of a graceful God affirm her personal value. Both empower her seeking protection, which affords her the opportunity to ponder the form of forgiveness for Juan that will emerge and which she will ultimately choose to enact with him. Her pathway to forgiveness includes two important factors: her need for protection and her freedom to choose to see Juan in a new light while ending their marriage or orchestrating with him a reconciliation, encompassing fundamental changes in each of them and their mutual relationship.

But not all who write on the subject of forgiveness would agree with what I am offering Rosa. Voices from the early Christian community and contemporary Christians would make forgiveness, in the form of reconciliation, a requirement. Sympathetically, we may say that variety abounds within the Christian understanding of life, although sarcastically, some might say a cacophony of voices yell at us about how to live.

Because of these varied and confusing voices about forgiveness, many persons have turned to the contemporary behavioral sciences for their answers. Seekers will find quality, sensitivity, and understanding in scientific approaches. I wish to state my appreciation for those who have thrown up their hands at, or washed their hands of, both scripture and theology. However, since I am grounded in the Christian faith, my mission here is to find a way to both affirm a vision of God and, through that vision, find caring answers for the knotty questions of life. I desire that especially for the Rosas of our world.

STANDING AT A CROSSROAD

I stand at a crossroad.
Only because I am safely protected
    can I do so.
I am able to think, weigh, and consider,
    without fear of personal harm.
Some say I am in a pathway
    bordered on both sides by thick bushes,
    having no choice but to follow
    the well-worn tracks before me.
However, I risk guardedly that I have a choice.
My intuition says so;
    my experience is less sure.

One path is to try again,
    to hold out hope for change,
    to continue investing,
    to live with uncertainty,
    to wait and see,
    to wonder when I will know,
    to wonder how I will know.
This path is to seek reconciliation.

A second path is to close our relationship,
    to end the partnership we created,
    to see the other in a new light,
    to begin the slow process of healing,
    to have certainty about an ending,
    to enter a series of unknowns ahead.
This path is to forgive without restoring.

No one can know what to do but me.
Nor can anyone begin walking for me.
I stand before a frightening judgment call.
I am inexperienced in this task.
Other voices beckon me to follow
    one path or the other.

Some with heavily weighted vested interest
    in how my choice will affect them.
Would that the voices would call me
    in only one direction,
      or express trust in my choosing.

The silent voices torment me the most,
    those for whom I am responsible.
My choice affects so many about me,
    my web of life may be radically changed,
    close relationships may be distanced,
    friendships may need to be rebuilt.
So many affect me, I affect so many.
Is it possible to take into account so many,
    and still know that the decision is mine?

How will I define myself in this moment?
What guides will I use in this moment?
I trust that whatever my choice,
I will not lose my relationship with grace.
I waiver between assurance and fear.
Yet I know that my relationship with You
    will never be the same.
My choice will also affect You.

The possibilities that You may offer to me
    will be different on the two paths.
On one I will receive wisdom about how
    to forgive and reconcile.
On the other I will receive knowledge
    of ending and forgiving.
Either way, Grace encircles me
    in the midst of surrounding uncertainty.
I know not yet which path I shall follow,
    but I do know Who will accompany me.

4

He Still Denies He Ever Touched Me

It was the late movie on television that brought it on. Rachel sat watching after Kylie was tucked in, and Dan had gone to bed early. She was catching a few minutes of relaxation, so precious to a young mother. Surprisingly, she found herself caught up in the story of a grandfather raising his young grandchild. Watching the scene where the girl crawled up into her grandfather's lap, Rachel found herself increasingly agitated, sweat beads forming on her forehead. As the grandfather began to read from the children's book, Rachel shocked herself by screaming, "Look out! Get down!"

Flashes of memory flooded her mind like a strobe light. Pictures came rushing like a tidal wave. It was the last she saw of the movie, for Rachel was overwhelmed in her own emotional drama. In her imagination it was Fred, her stepfather, who was reading, not the grandfather. She saw the large comfortable chair, heard words about children spending the day at the zoo, and felt a choking sensation in her throat. It was as though she could not move, being held by some strong invisible force. Her attempts to squirm away were stopped; her efforts to cry out were silenced.

Tears rushed down her face; her entire body throbbed rhythmically; she clenched her fists and beat at the large pillows on the sofa; she whimpered: "No reading! No trip to the zoo!" Too many reminders came flowing out that were part of the game that Fred played with his stepdaughter. All were signals of danger. Agitated, terrorized, and panic-stricken, Rachel was caught up in what she thought she had set aside many years before. Her stepfather had sexually abused her for many years.

During that sleepless night on the sofa, she experienced the dramatic difference between knowing something and feeling it. At age thirteen Rachel had said a determined "No!" to Fred, speaking with great power as she gripped a hammer in her hand. He stopped! She had decided after many false starts that at this special birthday she would begin a new life. No longer would she live two lives, one public, the other secret. Fred would be around, but she would avoid him whenever possible and treat him courteously for her mother's sake. However, her life would be oriented outside her family home. The five years prior to graduation and leaving home were challenging to live out and difficult to endure, but Rachel was a determined person. She vowed just as strongly to shelve the whole matter, convinced that those hurts were in the past, and she had to move on. She would start anew, and she did. Her guiding words were to let the past be the past.

But this night taught her differently. Past and present merged into a collage of frightening pieces. Her perplexing gagging response at the dentist's office blended with events occurring in the comfortable chair. Her near-panic at having a regular pap smear and the necessary pelvic exams during her pregnancy merged with the pain she felt during what Fred called their special times together. On this night all that she had so carefully placed on the shelf was now being blown off by gale winds.

As the long night wore on, the random kaleidoscope of images and feelings began to fit more into a picture of her own story. Some order began to merge with the initial chaos. Her mother and father had divorced when Rachel was only two. Maxine remarried three years later when Rachel was entering preschool. Fred was a master carpenter in their small community, known as the person to hire if you wanted a quality job done, for he was a meticulous follower of the old maxim "measure twice, cut once."

Maxine was a registered nurse who had worked for years in the obstetrics ward of their small regional hospital. With few specialists in this rural area, Maxine had caringly guided many young women through their labor while they waited for the harried doctor to arrive for the delivery. Frequently she would point out to Rachel "her babies" as they met young people at the grocery store or church. Rachel's teachers and other parents considered her blessed to have two highly respected persons as her parents.

Jeb and Sarah, children of Fred's from an earlier marriage, spent weekends with them once a month and several weeks during the summer. In her younger years it felt good to have them visit, since Rachel could tag along with the older, more privileged pair. The negative side was that their father's attention went their way, but there was an obvious positive side for Rachel to gain relief by moving farther out of sight for a few short days.

In the more routine days, three of them made up the family. Fred went to work early for his construction jobs, ending his day in the late afternoon, while Maxine had always worked the "three-to-eleven" shift. Except for a brief time period, this meant that child care was covered, but it also meant ample opportunity for Fred to molest Rachel with little chance of being detected. Winter evenings were the worst for her, darkness falling early and taking away any opportunity to play outdoors in the neighborhood. It should be no surprise that Rachel dreaded those cold winter months.

She found ways to stay away from home as long as possible, joining the Blue Birds, 4-H, and church youth programs. Whenever possible she would arrange to go home after school with a friend, hoping that dinner might be included, delaying her return home. A second-best would be to invite a friend home with her, but no matter what Rachel planned, there was that evening time when only she and her stepfather were there. Bathing time, story time, and tucking in were all dangerous arenas to a small child and developing girl. Nothing she could do, short of feigning illness or forcing her mind to leave the scene, would keep Rachel safe. In fact, headaches, nausea, and fever came with seemingly unknown causes. She was plagued by violent nightmares and at times walked in her sleep. Rachel was not aware of the connection between the night dreams, the illnesses, and the molesting; but, even if she had been, it would have made little difference. She had been told firmly and repeatedly that these times were a special secret between them.

To tell would take away the magic and love shared by parent and child.

As a teenager Rachel enjoyed the attention boys gave her but felt tense and tight as a young man would hold her hand, put his arm around her, or urge her to share a kiss. At the school dances she was always relieved when the fast numbers were played, so that she had distance from her partner and freedom of movement. If ever there was a push and pull, it was Rachel and her feelings toward boys. Fortunately, it was rare that she thought about the double life she had lived. In the "April loves" of her life, Rachel had little notion of how she was supposed to feel. In the lively talk about boys at the late-night slumber parties she was especially quiet, sensing that what she felt would be considered strange or silly. Listening to her friends made it easy for Rachel to believe that something was wrong with her.

Rachel followed in her mother's footsteps as she enrolled in the X-ray technician course at the nearby community college. It was while working at the hospital that she met Dan, a young deputy in the county sheriff's department. After nearly a year of courtship they married, and within two years Kylie was born. Life tasted good as they moved into parenting and continued their two career family. Rachel's parents lived twenty miles away in the next small town, so visiting was frequent and pleasant.

Plans for their family were progressing well, in spite of having a number of goals yet to meet and knowing that certain areas of their life could be more satisfying. This terrifying night brought dramatic change to any plans.

In the early morning hours Rachel decided to write. She had written many times in her secret diary to clear her mind and clarify her thinking. As she scrawled her intense feelings, she found herself repeatedly addressing her stepfather and gradually realized she was composing a letter to him. She would write him, bringing out the entire story, and confront him with exactly what he had done to her. Her hand moved rapidly across the paper, pausing at times before a new burst of energy guided the pen again. Finally, it was done. She felt utterly exhausted and laid her head back on the sofa pillow. As the first rays of the morning sun crept into the living room, she was awakened by Dan touching her shoulder. Startled, she sat up abruptly.

Deeply disturbed at what he saw, Dan questioned Rachel about what was happening. She wept and reached out for him. Hardly able to speak, she pointed to the letter. His eyes rapidly scanned the scribbled words, his distress growing with each page. As he laid down the last page, he yelled, "I'll blow him away!" Rachel covered his mouth, "No, no, Dan this is my thing. I've got to deal with it!"

In the early morning hours two persons in love sat and talked about an evil that had deeply affected one and now fully affected two. For one it was known but set aside; for the other it was new and explosive. Their talk concluded with Dan agreeing that Rachel needed to pursue her own answer. She would send the letter.

Weeks later the telephone call came from Fred at a time when he knew Dan would be on duty. He addressed Rachel in that familiar, pleasant voice. He said that he felt so badly for her that all the news hype of the day had caused her to misread their special times together. Too many talk shows, magazine articles, and sensational books made this the latest fad. Being bombarded by all that media talk would make one think that every woman in the country had been abused.

Rachel attempted to counter his words, but as so many times before, found herself overwhelmed. She asked if he had read her letter carefully. She spoke of the game they played about children visiting the zoo. Fred replied that they both had loved those stories and asked that she not turn them into anything other than two caring people sharing a lovely child's fantasy. Rachel was stilled by his adamant denial. Those acts that had so emotionally engulfed her recently, he claimed, must have been a figment of her own imagination. He expressed concern for her and promised that he would pray for her recovery. Rachel felt as if she had been abused again, camouflaged by the old sickeningly sweet words.

Rachel was defeated but she was not finished! She and Dan talked about the telephone conversation. In the months following there came many days of quiet reflection, punctuated by periods of intense agitation. The approaching of the Thanksgiving holiday brought an end to the reflection. Rachel could not imagine being at the family dinner at her parents' home, acting as though nothing had happened. Picturing that incredible scene empowered her to the next action: She and Dan would talk with her mother and Fred. Surely in this setting he would not be able to smoothly slide out of the accusations.

On a chilly November day they met on neutral ground, a nearby restaurant. Rachel screwed up her courage and spoke again, this time asking if her mother had read the letter. She had. Turning to Fred, Rachel firmly stated that she needed a confession, an apology, and financial help in seeking a professional counselor. Fred's earlier pleasantness turned to anger. "I'm not going to put up with this! What are you trying to do? No, it didn't happen and that's it! Why don't you get a life and stop grubbing around in the past? Grow up!" With those words he stomped out of the restaurant. Dan used great restraint not to follow him to parking lot. Quelling those feelings, he sat still.

Rachel sat facing her mother, a new, unpleasant quietness between them. When Maxine finally spoke, she uttered heavy, measured words. She was caught between two persons she loved and was devastated that this issue now divided her husband and her daughter. Rachel was quick to reply that the gulf had been there since she was five, only it was then secret. Her mother had no way to know what was the truth, for she wanted to believe both. Her stance would be to remain neutral, loving each. Her deepest desire was that there be some way to bridge the gulf. Rachel saw no possibility unless her stepfather owned up to what he had done. She could not be in the same room or sit at the same table with one who abused and lied. Their relationship was over due to his actions. Any other solution would perpetuate her agonizing years of living a lie, carrying out two lives.

Dan and Rachel drove home in silence, engrossed in their own thoughts. Dan knew that the statute of limitations was over, so that legal action was not possible. Even if it were possible to bring suit, he had witnessed the devastation to all parties in the "he said, she said" cases in the courtroom.

Rachel pondered the explosive consequences of the secret now out in the light. She wondered how she and her mother would create a more limited relationship and how she would explain to Kylie that they could not go to Grandpa's house. Would she tell close friends why they were not spending holidays with her family or again live in secrecy?

The multitude of questions could not be answered by herself. She decided to seek professional help and a group of supportive women. Somehow it would have been much more simple to continue to live the secret; but, in the midst of the confusion, Rachel at least felt whole and real for the first time in many years.

My story of Rachel is offered to represent persons who have been sexually abused by those persons who should protect them and ensure their well-being. The radical hurt imposed grows from this discrepancy as well as the early age of the victim. The total being of the child is undermined by this early abuse. It is particularly difficult to search out the relevance of forgiveness for these severely abused persons. The usual stages of forgiveness clearly do not apply: offense, confession, apology, and reconciliation.

I should note the hesitancy with which I, a male, dare to write about the experiences of a female. On the other hand, to omit this significant realm of life needing forgiveness would be unacceptable to me. I enter into it both with humility and with the consultation of my spouse, who counsels with abused women. I have drawn this story from a composite of situations where I have companioned women recovering from molestation. If the story of Rachel needs to be modified in certain areas, such as making the offended person a male, I am encouraging those changes and remain hopeful that the revised and more realistic story may offer an opportunity to apply a new vision of forgiveness. Given those admitted limitations, I wish now to apply the vision to this story, hoping that it may also be relevant to revised stories.

No reconciliation was possible for Rachel. To do so under the present conditions would be to prolong the secrecy and the lies, a continuation of abuse to Rachel. The basis for reconciliation was not present on Fred's side: admitting, taking responsibility, apologizing, repenting, commiting to seek professional help for himself, and agreeing to financially assist her to seek professional help. Instead we have an offender manipulating the offended once again by saying that she is wrong, misguided, and lying.

Rachel chose not to go to her parents' home again or to any event where Fred would be present, including birthdays, anniversaries, family reunions, or holiday gatherings. This choice would serve as an expression of the new honesty, as well as protecting Kylie and any future children from potential abuse. Her guide was, simply, I won't have him here; I won't go there; I will see my mother alone.

Accepting this loss for herself, her husband, and her daughter was a continuing and difficult task for her. Each birthday and holiday appearing on the calendar reopened the wound again. She had lost the normalcy enjoyed by many extended families.

Reconciliation was not possible; neither was the process of seeing Fred in a new light successful. In her many efforts to find a common humanity with her stepfather she crashed repeatedly into his selfish, forceful, and deceptive qualities. Try as she might, she could not dig deeply enough to find the good; peeling the layers of the onion revealed only the negative. She had heard the advice to "hate the sin, love the sinner," but it seemed beyond her to separate the person from the years of actions he initiated. Were the actions not permeated through and through by who he was? She tried to use the euphemism "He did the best he could," but she ultimately rejected it as basically untrue. He had not tried his best by anyone's standards. She discovered over a long period of time that she could pray for his well-being, leaving the knowledge of what that might mean to the wisdom of God.

Protection was a necessity for Rachel, as it had been for Rosa, facing domestic violence. Whenever reconciliation is not an option, protection appears as a requirement to safeguard one's personal well-being. Forgiveness is not to be engaged in at the expense of one's own self. While martyrdom has a rich tradition in Christian history, suffering is to be endured for a greater purpose. To simply allow an offender to continue abusing or to require that the offended live a lie does not qualify for martyrdom. Rachel's protection is appropriate, although it exacts a hurtful loss for her.

With these several pathways closed, the primary path of forgiveness for the sexually abused person is to focus on her own healing, while wrestling with the natural tendency to become embittered about life itself. The precarious nature of this pathway is that it becomes a lifetime walk with many unknown curves, rather than a short road with a clear ending in sight. So many of the issues around which healing are needed come around as regularly as dates on the calendar. This is a potent reason for needing a caring companion on the journey.

Let us return to the issue of the rights we expect in our daily lives. Sexual abuse violates the basics. Above all we assume the right that our bodies should be our own and be guided by our own will.

Likewise, we hold it to be a right that parents will foster the growth of children and protect them from danger. Both rights are violated by sexual abuse. Rights fail us. Returning to the vision of God offered here, only encircling grace is unfailing.

As a society we affirm the rights of children, but when those rights are violated, there is need for more than the adage that "life is not fair." The abused person knows that only too well, imprinted upon the tissue of her body. Hope lies rather in going beyond the adage, which states a partial truth, to the Graceful One who is always present in the midst of radical unfairness, continually advocating for us.

Rachel's healing included questioning where God was during those many occasions of abuse. Frequently persons throw over their belief in God because no divine power rescued them in their times of crying need. The question of how God could have allowed this violence to occur is central and valid. The vision of a God who is persuasive allows the abused to continue to believe that God cared about her and felt with her while offering possibilities of goodwill for all parties in those bleak moments. One crucial aspect of healing, then, for Rachel is to re-image an all-powerful God, who either caused or allowed her abuse for some mysterious and unknown reason or because of indifference, to an ever-encircling God who is intimate, graceful, and persuasive. From the divine as distant and indifferent or powerful and puzzling, healing moves toward a divine, graceful intimacy. To paraphrase Harry Emerson Fosdick, God moves from being part of the problem to being part of the solution.

Her healing occurs not once, but numerous times. We may accompany Rachel as she encounters the many monsters on her journey, much like those that faced Odysseus on his odyssey, Pilgrim on his progress, or Dante in his inferno.

A basic and pervasive problem is the feeling that the world is not a safe place. This feeling is often a sense of generalized anxiety that is not attached to any particular person or object. Fear is simply present most of the time and keenly present at certain times. Her abuse occurred at such a young age that fear of the particular person and the specific places fanned out easily to encompass all of life.

A segment of that fear is that she will be found out. To allow others to know what she is really like within in contrast to the public self she exhibits is unbearable. Living a secret, a dual life, is like a spring bubbling forth bringing fear from her depths. Around her the world is filled with fear, and she is filled with fear from within.

Trust in another is damaged. While Rachel knew in her heart that Dan loved her completely, she could not eradicate the gnawing fear that at any time his love could turn to force and control, the sequence she experienced with her stepfather. Kindness, caring, words of love might transform easily to firmness, control, and force as her wants receded, his grew. She felt so guilty about this obsessive thought that pervaded even their moments of closeness that she had never dared share it with Dan.

Mistrust blended with her confusion about love. Where love and tenderness should be felt, she felt tightness and pain. In moments of mutual caressing and touching that she knew should bring her pleasure, she felt the opposite. To feel any satisfaction, she imagined that she was a prisoner being tortured while tied to a wall. Thus, sexual intimacy that she knew should be a positive bonding experience became dreaded because of the mental gymnastics she would go through to achieve the desired feeling.

Even putting all this effort into what should be spontaneous play, Rachel would often sense a "click," whereupon she would lose feeling in her lower body. She came to fear the act of penetration in the beginning of intercourse, for in that moment she became numb. She could not predict on which occasion the numbness would appear. Her will could not reach the switch.

With these struggles inherent in her touching relationship with Dan, it was no surprise that Rachel would hesitate to reach out for affection or initiate a sexual embrace. Often Dan felt rejected and unwanted. Rachel denied those feelings and affirmed her desire for closeness, once again promising to move toward him, promises that were either not always kept or carried out by effort rather than desire. She did want closeness, but not the turmoil she faced in that intimacy. In these struggles it was most difficult to restrain her intense hatred toward her stepfather, the promoter of this muddled confusion. Her early choices for dealing with unwanted touching were still in place, now deeply entrenched habits. She worried that one day Dan would reach total exasperation and leave, taking with him the one love Rachel could not afford to be without in the face of so many other losses.

A greater terror lurked deep within Rachel, a fear that she was a "bad seed." In moments of deep despair, she blamed her own seductive desires as the cause of it all. Had she started it? Had she secretly wished for everything that had happened? Was she base and lustful? Even more disturbing was the threat that she might unknowingly impose these sexual desires upon Kylie. She wondered if she could trust herself to protect her own daughter, questioning the very core of her being. Surfacing and confronting these frightening questions would be later tasks in her pathway to forgiveness.

Struggling with her parenting of Kylie would easily lead Rachel to ponder her relationship with her own mother. A host of feelings would emerge as she thought back across those years. How was she to think of her mother during those secret events? Did her mother know and look the other way? Was she too afraid to lose her husband to confront him? As a nurse, should she not have seen the signs of abuse? Were her family members too close to allow her professional perspective to emerge? Did she naively believe it could never happen to them? Her mother maintained that she suspected nothing. Rachel needed to believe her mother, to see her as a caring parent, but at times mistrust won out over these needs. Rachel had two difficult tasks, to see her mother's place in the past and to develop a limited relationship with her in the present.

A major obstacle in her path to forgiveness was the glaring truth that she was gypped by life. Rachel would never be the person she might have been. The violence came so early in her life that her growth veered in the directions of fear, mistrust, and self-doubt. Moreover, she was required by the circumstances to give attention to issues that should have come later. Energy that might have gone for growth and blossoming was sapped totally for protection and survival. The limitations that were forged in those early fiery moments became central in her character and personality. Daily she would face the gap between who she might have been and who she was.

Facing this gap brought with it a sense of unfairness, hurt, blame, anger, and at times, rage. To come to the point of repeatedly accepting this loss was a laborious process. The qualities that were often simply taken for granted by others, Rachel was able to achieve occasionally.

It would be easy for Rachel to take the wide and well-traveled trail toward cynicism and bitterness with life. She could summarize her bitterness easily: He did, I pay! The desire for justice shouted loudly but was not answered. Thinking from the worldview of rights we deserve, she had every right to walk that trail. In these moments the whisperings of the Graceful Companion were essential. That trail sign marked bitterness beckoned frequently, and it was with determination that she kept on the path to forgiveness.

Her greatest struggle, also kept the most secret, centered on whether Fred might be right. Was she in the final sense a liar, a fabricator, a great storyteller? Herein was her ultimate self-doubt. Could she trust herself to know her own experiences? After all, she had never put the abuse into words as we do with most significant experiences. Were they finally only fantasy? No other person knew about them and confirmed their truthfulness. The ways we usually come to trust our own experiences, saying them aloud to others, were closed to Rachel. The only one who could confirm, in fact, denied. An adult discounted the words of a child.

She had learned well to cooperate, not to confront. In the power differential of the abusing moments, she was truly powerless, helpless, and overwhelmed. Little opportunity presented itself to fight back, resist, scream, or run. Early attempts at control were quickly squelched, as she did not have the power of an adult to consent or decline.

The skills she created back then to survive with him now worked against her in the requirement that she confront and disagree with that same person.

Strength and determination were necessary for her to trust her own memory and her own present feelings, leading to: Yes, it happened. I do know what I know.

Again, forgiveness became the long path of healing herself while remaining protected from the abuser. I believe it is the unusual person who can walk that path alone. Professionals and persons who have also suffered sexual abuse are critical to the recovery of well-being. My interest is in adding the importance of the Graceful Companion to that journey. One's capacity to deal with the mammoth tasks along the way is greatly enhanced by a relationship with grace and a creation imbued with grace.

Scripture appears silent on this particular form of violence, perhaps because of the patriarchy that permeates its pages. The man had ultimate authority over both women and children, his will being the rule. Jesus does not directly address this problem in his parables or sayings, except as the gospel writer portrays him admonishing the disciples for sending children away, and elevating them as a model of the kingdom of heaven.

Most of relevant scripture points to a paradigm of repentance and forgiveness, which does not fit here due to the absence of the offender's admitting guilt and asking pardon.

Reconciliation is not possible under the present conditions. Gradually seeing the offender in a new light does not bring the offended one to any sense of common humanity or empathy with the offender. Following the empathic pathway, again, seems contingent on a new decision by the offender. It may be that sometime in the distant future, Rachel might see the positive facets of her stepfather. Walking into the buildings of her hometown would be an ever-present reminder of this man's sense of skill and artistry with wood. Ironically, she might wish that he had had as much respect and caring for her as he did for the precious hardwoods with which he crafted an interior.

The clearest pathway of forgiveness is that of entering a process of healing herself, informed by the full awareness that the grace of the universe fully desires her reaching that goal. Honesty looms large in the struggle toward healing, honesty with her stepfather, her mother, her husband, her daughter, her friends, and especially herself. The freedom to do so is one of the basic gifts of this path to forgiveness. No longer must she ignore and deny what is true, as painful as that truth may be. Losses result, but they are not as damaging as those earlier losses through deception. Now she can gain ground. Problems can be faced, felt, and resolved. Rachel can move from the inner dividedness, confusion, and denial into a realm of openly dealing with the worst she can remember.

Slowly and gradually, Rachel may also be able to consider other identities besides that of a survivor of sexual abuse. Herein is the tension of knowing that she will never be who she might have been and entertaining the idea that new surprising identities may unfold for her. The necessity of spending so much energy and time on her own healing naturally makes it difficult to look beyond herself. Her danger of remaining in the imposed and fixed identity is that she will be deaf to any new possibilities for her life. In the midst of this tension and in its proper time, grace whispers of the new becoming she might enter. Just as healing encompasses a lifetime of unfolding tasks, so do the lurings toward new possibilities continually come. Grace lures her, and all of us, toward ever-expanding empathy with the complexities of our own depth and the breadth of creation.

There are authors who focus at some depth upon the healing from sexual abuse from the perspective of the behavioral sciences. My primary contrast with them is that their approach is psychological whereas mine is theological. Our similarity is acknowledging the long, difficult process of healing. I affirm that the companionship of the Graceful One is immensely empowering on this difficult path of forgiveness.

PERSONAL WORTH

I have so little of myself
    that belongs to me.
Every facet of me has been violated.
My will, my desires, my body,
    my knowing, my experiences,
    my independence, my dreams.
In the deepest parts of my being
    is anything uniquely me?
Or am I a hollow chameleon?

I struggle to trust myself and others.
I have thoughts and feelings,
    and doubt them.
Do I think that idea
    or am I pleasing another?
Did that really happen
    or was it only my imagination?
Is that what I truly feel
    or something I should feel?

I want to be told what to do,
    yet I cling to my independence.
I wonder if my inner wisdom left me
    or never had a chance to develop.
Others appear to know
    what they know with certainty.
I undermine, question, and debate
    each emerging finding.
Where is my center?
Do I fully fit together
    or am I scattered pieces?

While the whirlwind goes on within
    I fear the world surrounding me.
There is little that I find certain
    and trustworthy.
I hear the words
    but question their truth.
I see the evidence
    but I am not convinced.
I am certain of danger
    and possible harm.
I want to be close
    but I do not know how.
I yearn to speak intimate words
    but sounds do not come forth.
I long for touching
    yet numb myself when I am embraced.
I know of your love for me
    and I fear your harming me.

Oh, why did this happen to me?
Why must I go on living
    in such imprisoning agony?
I hate the one who forced me
    into this prison.
In my dreams I raise my sword
    and exact my revenge.

Justice is served, right is restored,
    but then I awaken in my cell.
Will no one advocate for me today,
    just as no one protected me then?
My search for justice
    ends in vain!
There is no way to make it right.
No portal opens offering what I deserved.

Will I simply remain damaged,
    and writhing in my private hell?
Lo, I sense a hand reaching toward me,
    a warmth encircling me,
    a cool breeze gently touching
    my fevered brow,
    a knowing acceptance shining upon me.
Could anyone draw near to such
    a troubled person as I?
Might anyone risk intimacy with
    one who distorts relationships?
Dare I trust this Presence when voices
    within cry out to be careful?
You will be manipulated!
    suffer harm!
    be fooled again!
    experience again your badness!
    fail once more!
    have your hopes dashed!

To remain safe I could stay in my cell,
    to risk I invite many dangers.
One I know well,
    the other is a stranger.
The whispers grow more loudly,
    the acceptance more uplifting.
Perhaps I will take one small step.
Yes!

5

We Haven't Seen Our Men
Since That Night

"The prisoners were Croats, Muslims and Albanians, that is, people of non-Serb nationality. Among the prisoners there were women and old men, men of over 60 and one who was 73. Prisoners were not being brought from the battlefields as captives but from their homes. Practically all of them had to go through various kinds of torture: beatings, being kept in closed, hot, suffocating premises, denied drinking water and denied the use of the toilet, as well as poor nutrition." (56)★

"The beatings were at the beginning done by special forces, from Serbia. Later the job was taken over by policemen who guarded us. They were local Serbs who carried out their jobs far more brutally than the special units men. They beat us with iron bars, wooden two-by-fours and truncheons, iron and rubber devices for beating, with their feet, and they were wearing military boots, with their fists and hands." (56)

"The victim was beaten over the head, neck, shoulders, back, chest, hips, feet, and arms, that is, over the entire body. Sometimes he

---

★All quotations and page numbers in this chapter are from Roy gutman, A Witness to Genocide (New York: Macmillan Publishing Company, 1993).

was beaten by one man, sometimes by three, and sometimes even 10 policemen at the same time. They usually beat us during the day-time, sometimes in the room where we were housed and sometimes in the yard. After torture like this, the victim was coverd with blood, over the head and back, and his back was blue and red from the blows." (56f.)

"I think the most horrible night was the one between the sev-enth and eighth of May when a Serbian Special Force squad came to the farmers cooperative storerooms in Crkvini…and shot 15 of the 45 people there. When the door of the storeroom was forcibly opened, we were ordered, without the lights being turned on, to line up along one side of the room, which we did speedily. (58)

"Another Special Force man shined a flashlight on us one by one, and the first Special Force man chose his victim, hitting him on the head with his gun and then shooting him and killing him. The people were collapsing on the floor in a heap, and blood was pour-ing across the concrete floor. When he finished his first round, he ordered the others who had survived to quickly line up on the other side of the room, which we did. He again began to choose and to shoot his victims. I know that in the second round he asked everybody their name and their occupation, and then he made his choice on those grounds, and then shot the people. About 15 people were left lying dead in that room. Around them on the concrete was a pool of their blood." (58f.)

"Then they moved us over to the third side of this room, and ordered the younger people to load the dead bodies on a truck, which had come up to the doorway. Then he told them to clean the blood off the floor, which they did. We spent that night in the same room." (A former prisoner at the Bosanski Samac detention camp, Slavonski Samac, Croatia, August 3, 1992). (59)

"They would say they are feeding the fish…The very worst day—and I saw it with my own eyes—was when I saw 10 young men laid out in a row. They had their throats slit, their noses cut off and their genitals plucked out. It was the worst thing I saw." (Zagreb, Croatia, August 2, 1992) (50f.).

"I didn't bury him….The river took him away….If the Drina River could only speak, it would say how many dead were taken away." Hasnija witnessed the execution of her husband, Nenad, from the terrace of her house outside Visegrad.

It was 7:30 a.m., June 24, and Nenad was returning from his overnight factory shift when the armed men in Serbian paramilitary uniforms spotted him. Nenad started running to the nearby riverbank, but the irregulars shot him dead on the spot. They dragged the corpse onto the bridge, then threw it into the green water of the Drina. (Miratovc, Yugoslavia, July 3, 1992) (24)

"I was an honest girl. I was a virgin. I gave it to someone who didn't deserve it. Someone whom I love deserves it. But not a savage." (Satka, age 20) (72)

"We all feel that we lost everything....We have been abandoned. We have been imperiled. Every woman, if she is raped, has to feel the same." (Heira, age 25) (72)

"He said we were the cleanest convoy that passed Caparde, the prettiest and most attractive, and that they couldn't let us pass because we were so beautiful....They would come by and tap us on the shoulder....They told everyone else that we had gone to 'fetch water.' Some of the girls came back two hours later. Some the next morning. And each of them sat down and cried." (Hejira, age 21) (71)

"I was raped every night." She asked one captor why they suddenly turned on them. "The answer was that he had to do it. He said, 'Because you are Muslims, and there are too many of you.' "

"Everyone who is with us now (other refugees) does not believe we were forced....And they think we are going to go with them (the Serbs) again. We can't imagine marriage as a normal thing. We know that the man will always be supicious." (Sevlata, age 18) (76)

"Only two nights I was not raped....I knew all of them who did it. They were my neighbors." (Ziba, age 18) (75–76)

On May 17, after Serbian forces entered the town, Fazlic, other elderly residents, women, and children were taken to the nearby village of Trnopolje. They spent two weeks in a detention center set up inside a sports hall. The able-bodied men and youths of Kozarac, including one of Fazlic's sons, were taken to Omarska. They have not returned. Muslim officials believe Omarska is a death camp.

"They demanded that he provide the names of all Muslim activists," Fazlic said. Ilijaz refused. "They (the military) took electric drills and bored them into their chests." The three children ages 1, 3, and 5, were impaled on spikes. "We saw it with our own eyes." (41)

In one concentration camp, a former iron-mining complex at Omarska in northwest Bosnia, more than a thousand Muslim and Croat civilians were held in metal cages without sanitation, adequate food, exercise, or access to the outside world....The prisoners at the camp...include the entire political and cultural elite of the city of Prijedor. Armed Serbian guards executed prisoners in groups of 10 to 15 every few days.... (44)

Meho, 63...was held in an ore loader inside a cage roughly 700 square feet, along with 300 other men awaiting processing by their captors....The metal superstructure contained cages stacked four high, separated by grates. There were no toilets, and prisoners had to live in their own filth, which dripped through the grates. (45) "...there was nowhere to lie down. You'd drowse off and fall against the next person." (48)

A guard at Omarska was quoted as saying: "We won't waste our bullets on them. They have no roof. There is sun and rain, cold nights, and beatings two times a day. We gave them no food and no water. They will starve like animals." (47)

Meho reported that they were threatened repeatedly: "They would say to us that for every Serb killed on the battlefield, we will take 300 of you." (48)

The mothers arrived in Tuzla on June 23, distraught about their missing daughters and traumatized by the journey, which began with another bus ride and ended with a forced 12-mile walk through a war zone on a road littered with human corpses and animal carcasses. Their daughters arrived four days later, after a forced walk across a mined road with several elderly people, a number of whom died en route, they said.

The young women were exhausted and in a state of shock....Most...had vaginal infections of staphyllococcus and other bacteria that originated in dirt or fecal matter...each is missing a father or a brother as well as the material basis of their lives. They are women in the prime of life, but few have anywhere to go; and the rapes have shaken their confidence. (71f.)

Apalling, unbelievably apalling! It is nearly impossible to read the personal accounts of those men, women, and youth who were victims of heinous crimes and witnesses to a systematic effort at genocide. The events are recent, most dated in 1992, and represent the Serbian effort at ethnic cleansing in Bosnia–Herzegovina, a part of the earlier Yugoslavia. I have shared the horror through their own direct experiences and descriptions. Many lives have been brutally taken, all lives have been radically broken, and a way of life left in ruins. Fathers, brothers, husbands were ripped away and horrendously tortured or murdered, wives were left bereaved widows and sonless mothers, daughters have lost the men in their lives and remain frightfully damaged by the numerous violations of their precious virginity.

The instances reported here are specifics in a class of events in which people are set against people, often, tragically, neighbor against neighbor. History is replete with these acts of oppression and genocide: Hebrews and Canaanites, Turks and Albanians, Stalinists and Soviets, Japanese and Chinese, Europeans and Native Americans, Tutsi and Hutu, Central Americans and Indians, Khmer Rouge and Cambodians, White Afrikaaners and Black Africans, and most vivid in my boyhood experience, the Nazi Third Reich and European Jews. I doubt that any continent or any period of history is without these tragic atrocities and brutality.

May forgiveness even be whispered here? Is there any way in which forgiveness is relevant to the horrors experienced in Bosnia or in any of these other historic tragedies? I would personally find it presumptuous to introduce the subject to the Muslim and Croatian persons who were quoted here. Rather, their critical needs would appear to be protecting their lives, cultivating farmland, securing a water supply, creating political boundaries, reestablishing a system of government, locating means of earning income, rebuilding homes, providing proper burial of their loved ones, grieving the horrendous loss of family members, and restoring some semblence of community in the absence of most men and in the presence of so many injured women.

Scars remain: empty chairs at the table, the picture on the fireplace mantel, the absence of an available marriage partner, the loss of father, mother, daughter, son, and the lack of previous work. Irreplaceable losses stalk the land and each hearth.

Yet, in the midst of such loss there remains a need for a word of hope. The question is what form hope might take for these particular violated and wounded people. It is with great humility that I even dare to consider the place of forgiveness in offering hope. Yet I feel compelled because of the unspeakable tragedy they endured and because the one whom I name God experienced the tragedy along with them. I must speak on behalf of the tenderness and compassion of Grace.

I begin by affirming that which I consider reality: God is with us in the form of intimacy, persuasion, and grace. Those wounded ones could tell us without question that rights are not guaranteed, for theirs were so fundamentally violated. Likewise, justice did not hold up for them, who have lived through the most extreme forms of injustice. Grace alone remains. No human rights were respected: life, property, freedom, the privacy of one's body. None! Henceforth, trust in the agreements among people will be held tentatively, acknowledging their extreme vulnerability.

I do not know whether any of the victims experienced grace in the midst of torture, deprivation, rape, or dying. I would affirm its presence even in the bloodiest of torture and the most painful moments of dying. I also affirm that the Graceful One was persuading all parties in every situation. However, I know that the need in those moments was for saving action, not persuasion. Where is the God of the universe when I need God? Why doesn't God send manna from heaven to us starving below, reach down and wrench the truncheon from the attacker's hand, distract the aim of the neighbor pointing the rifle, rip open the door of the stifling, crowded cage, or restrain the rapist from violating? Yes, there was need for an all-powerful force who would intervene on behalf of the oppressed. In the newer vision, we do not know that manner of God.

God persuades all, the oppressor and the oppressed, the attacker and the victim. In the midst of the horror, this report may offer a glimmer of grace. "...some young women said they had been taken to a house and not raped but were instructed to tell others that they had been raped."(69) Far more often, however, the whispers of God luring toward acts of compassion were blatantly ignored. The drive toward destruction and death won.

God creates with whatever is available; God persuades whoever is present; God offers novel lures even in the face of the atrocious but powerful belief in ethnic superiority. God whispers of a greater vision in the face of the distorted vision now seen.

A path toward forgiveness that I would offer is accepting God as persuasively present, in contrast to raging toward God or turning in disgust from God for not saving them in their dire need. To be consumed with anger toward the divine or to face life without grace is to lose the most crucial resource in a wasteland with scant resources. To convict God of complicity with these crimes against humanity is to lose a Mysterious Friend who accompanies them. I urge a holding close to the Compassionate One who felt with them every blow, every cut, every pang of hunger, every dying breath.

With a graceful God as traveling companion, there may well be three paths toward forgiveness: protecting their lives and community, recovering from their unspeakable trauma, and accepting the present conditions of their lives. These paths are filled with such complexity and difficulty as to comprise a lifetime journey. I am not assuming that persons will complete one, then go on to another, but that there will be a cyclic process in which all are addressed time and again without full closure on any.

I am proposing here, as I did with the issue of domestic violence, that protection from the aggressor is a crucial part of forgiveness. I do so with the full knowledge that it seems like the opposite of drawing near and reconciling. Those laudable and positive goals of reconciliation are probably not possible when responding to such horror and may await their fruition in God's heavenly community. A portion of the journey, then, is to build whatever degree of protection is possible.

While many would say it was too late, the international community decided on the intervention of a United Nations peacekeeping force. At this writing those military forces are still in place, making it difficult to know yet the effects of their withdrawal. The political process of determing boundaries, holding elections, and reestablishing government will be accomplished in coordination with the troop withdrawal. Protection is needed for recovery and healing to occur, for otherwise all energy flows into anxious watching and perpetual guarding. The protections offered by the international community and the returning internal community form a necessary step toward forgiveness. To do whatever is necessary to stay alive and unharmed is the highest priority. All other possibilities rest entirely upon that beginning.

Two pathways often taken toward forgiveness are closed in the aftermath of this genocide. The first is reconciliation, which would appear ludicrous to the victims of another group's violence, and the second is empathizing with the attacker. There is no basis for beginning reconciliation in that the Serbs have not felt remorse, stated an apology, asked for forgiveness, turned from their brutality, or offered reparation. Perhaps future generations may be able to build a bridge between Serbs, Croats, and Muslims, but presently the wounds appear too deep.

On the other pathway, increasing empathy would bring the victims to know the Serbs as persons who embody the belief in ethnic purity and whose well-being is based upon the total absence of the victims. That the victims might grow to feel a common humanity with the offender who believes that the world would be better off without them and wishes them dead seems a fruitless approach to take. One people cannot feel a unity with the desire of another people to destroy them. No, these two pathways are simply not available to the devastated ones!

We return, then, to protection, recovery, and acceptance. The processes of protection and recovery would seem to grow together. Healing themselves is a rocky and uncertain way in itself. There are dramatic physical wounds to heal. The lingering aftereffects on the health of imprisoned persons would be horrendous: enduring near starvation; facing the brunt of the elements without shelter; lacking proper sanitation, medical, or dental care; sleeping upright in suffocating circumstances, combined with the bleeding and bruising of soft tissue and the brokenness of skeletal bones from two brutal beatings a day. Survivors were maimed and disabled in the present, with a morbid sense that the syptoms would only worsen with the aging process.

Many women and girls who were forced to walk the mine-laden roads would live now with a lost limb. Young women would face the physical wounds and infections of repeated rapes. Children would be as vulnerable as their parents and elder siblings to the wounds of warfare. Healing of the physical body becomes a critical step toward new life.

The psychic and spiritual wounds loom just as large. War leaves the indelible imprint of trauma. American soldiers who were not facing genocide have experienced what has been diagnosed as "shell

shock," "battle fatigue," and "post traumatic stress disorder," depending upon the particular war in which they fought: World War I,
World War II, or the Vietnam Conflict. In warfare it is well known
that the greatest tragedy befalls the civilians: the elderly, the women,
and the children. The trauma of soldiers is magnified for the civilian.
The children are damaged so deeply because they have not yet developed sophisticated methods of coping with life. Their trauma is
naturally shared with the parents, most often a surviving mother or
grandmother, who must then cope for both herself and another.

We know also of "survivor's guilt," the critique of oneself for
living while so many others have died. There comes the search, Why
me? Accompanying it is the sense of not deserving the gift of life
that has been taken from others. I can imagine the inner torment of
the young woman who is able to marry while for many of her
friends their young men are simply absent. With whom will she
celebrate?

The aftermaths of trauma cry out for healing: despair, broken
sleep, hyperalertness, pervasive anxiety, hopelessness, depression,
numbness, immobilization, terrorizing flashbacks, memory loss, and
radical mistrust. No doubt books are yet to be written describing
the arduous healing process of an individual, family, or community.
It is only in its particularity that the fullness of the healing process
may be appreciated. Some brokenness is irreversible, some may be
modified, and some transformed. There is no question that the individual, family, and community will never be the same.

Recovery takes many forms, and one of greatest importance,
and equally great difficulty, is the acceptance of the situation as it is
in the present. Their lives are radically different than prior to the
ethnic massacre. Two powerful inner forces compete with one another: remembering what was before and accepting what is now.
Expectations have been shattered, dreams have become nightmares,
hopes have been dashed. Life now is without one or more family
members or without prospects of a marriage. Women who centered
their energy on spouse and children may now face a void or heavy
responsibilities of parenting without any support. Men are disfig-
ured, ill, and maimed, if alive at all. Neighbors and friends are absent
or are living as fragmented families. Homes, businesses, community
centers, churches, mosques, hospitals, and farms stand in ruin, crying
out the need to be rebuilt. Most leaders of their guiding institutions

of business, banking, medicine, religion, agriculture, and sports are dead, systematically sought out and killed. Ashes, nothing but ashes! How, oh how, does one accept this?

What is possible when standing in a pile of ashes, on the soil of newly dug graves? All, at times, would surely say, Nothing! No hope lies in this land. Remembering brings surging rage, vengeance, despair, and hurt. Recalling brings profound grief and cries for justice. Recalling expectations, childhood dreams, youthful hopes carries wrenching pain. Can persons move at all? Is there anything beyond the depressing and overwhelming void? It is into this exact situation that the voice of Grace speaks. Feeling with those who stand in ashes and on graves, new possibilities emerge that speak of hope and life. The new whispers may be unheard because of the tremendous power of anger, anguish, despair, and vengefulness. Grace may not be heard because of the profound cry for justice. The persuasive voice may not be heard above the forceful feelings enveloping the victims of atrocities. However, the call to recognize the current situation just as it is begins ever so slightly to contrast with the pain resulting from tragedy.

Forgiveness in the form of living in the present may well be a lifetime task. All the losses, the physical brokenness, the shattered dreams, may be gradually accepted while searching each arising moment for any tiny sign of the new.

Those throughout the planet who align with Grace will encircle these persons on their painful journey with prayer for their well-being. And in the midst of this journey of these decimated people, there may arise a unique person who may contemplate quietly the possibility of willing the well-being of the oppressors.

God's Ever-Present Encircling Grace

I contemplate grace,
    a Presence who gives unconditionally
    to all who reside in the universe,
    regardless of their form and being.
Whispering from within of the new,
    offering that which is beautiful,

calling each to greater complexity,
    luring all to increased intensity,
    challenging each to wider vision,
    desiring for all a tender compassion.
I look outward as far as I can see
    with human eye or scientific glass,
    beholding the planets of our system
    and the spheres of galaxies beyond,
    wondering if there be a place
    where grace is not to be found.
And I see none.

I map the cultures of the world,
    asking if grace persuades all peoples
    regardless of my opinion of them,
    or the judgment of history upon them,
    or the labels society places upon them,
    or their virtues, or their vices,
    or whether they even know of grace.
I affirm none are left outside the circle.

I look backward as far as I can see,
    questioning if there was a time
    when grace was not persuading
    throughout this expanding universe.
Peering at the smallest of the small
    through the prisms gifted us by science,
    and the largest of the large
    through the carbon dating of remains
    of those who once considered this home,
I ponder how grace called them
    beyond the water to the dry land
    and lured them to crawl, then walk.
I wonder how grace played with them
    and delighted in each new step forward
    toward becoming more complex and beautiful.
I write in my laboratory notebook:
    We are all members of the family of grace.

I ask my imagination to look ahead
    as far beyond as I can possibly comprehend,
    questioning again if grace will be found
    in whatever futures we may design
    beyond my own personal death,
    and the death of those whose names I know,
    toward generations yet to come
    to inhabit millennia yet to unfold,
    taking in all the predictions of cataclysms
    of overpopulation, global warming,
    resistant bacterial strains, alien warfare,
    rain forest depletion, atomic holocaust,
    ecological collapse, soil depletion,
    and the one thing that I know is that
    whatever is left and whoever has survived,
    grace will be luring those to newness.

I peer at that which I am told
    we cannot bear to look at
    my own death,
    wondering about that mysterious experience
    that unfolds beyond our own control
    and which bids us give up our all,
    trading everything for the unknown,
    convulsing and gasping desperately
    for the last breath of life or
    gently and tenderly letting go of
    the life that silently ebbs from us.
Will grace hold my hand in this
    awesome moment of transformation?
Will grace guide me to some form
    of adventure yet to unfold?
I do believe it to be so!

So, as I stand upon the Earth,
    I am upheld by those who went before
    who were persuaded by grace.

As I look back at the history of creation
    and my own personal history
    I am rooted in those who were
    called by grace.
As I see those beside me in the present
    I am accompanied by those who
    are daily enriched by grace.
As I look forward toward unknown futures
    I am lured by transforming grace.
    I am encircled by Grace!
We are encircled by Grace!

6

They're Just Gonna Shut 'er Down!

VICKI: It feels like someone kicked me right in the gut!

JOANNE: Right!

BILL: I still can't believe what I heard.

TAMI: I'm numb.

GREG: Yeah, and by October 1. That's not even two months!

ROB: I had to hold myself down. I was ready to go up there and punch him out!

VICKI: What're we gonna do? What ever are we gonna do?

GREG: That's the sixty-four dollar question, all right.

TAMI: But this line's been going for sixty years. Mom worked it all her life.

BILL: Both my mom and dad, too. And now Rita and I won't see any paycheck at all.

JOANNE: And they're gonna haul this stuff all the way to Nevada. It just doesn't add up for me.

TAMI: Well, I guess we should know it doesn't have to make sense. Look where our logging and fishing went.

JOANNE: Yeah, but I thought we could count on the cranberries.

BILL: Guess we all did, like it's part of the landscape.

VICKI: That's it. Like you could trust it to hang around.

ROB: Damn, I still can't believe it. You know I was gonna work a couple more years, hang it up, sell my house and move near the kids. Can you imagine what my place will be worth in a ghost town? Ninety-five people out of work. I probably won't be able to give it away!

TAMI: That is really sad, Rob. Really sad!

GREG: Well, it just burns my hide. That's what it does to me.

BILL: Just look at us sitting around this table. How many of us had grandparents who lived here? All but you, Rob!

VICKI: Guess this place has always been home. Where would I go if I left here? Nevada, they say! Why, I've never even been near the place.

GREG: Who wants the sagebrush. Give me the rain any day!

JOANNE: And to think we just signed our lives away to get that new lot.

TAMI: I know how much you've been planning on that.

VICKI: Speaking of mortgages, what about Glenda and the new preschool she was getting ready to start. Boy, she and Roy will be left hanging out to dry.

BILL: And we just bought that new RV. So, we sell it, but drive it around the block and its worth thousands less.

ROB: OK, how are they going to choose who goes and who stays? Now you seventy over here still have a job. Sorry you ninety-five are out on the street. Are they gonna draw straws or put names in a hat— cutting a line between our families and friends? How are the have-nots going to feel about the haves?

TAMI: It's not a pretty picture. It sets people against each other just when we were getting it together. Like that new school levy passing and finally getting those two doctors to fill the vacant clinic.

BILL: So we'll be the newest rural slum. I can see the weeds growing around the park and the potholes in the streets. We'll lose teachers. Cut down that many kids and the tax base and we can't afford to keep 'em.

GREG: I really wonder how many folks are already maxed out on their plastic. I can just picture the new list of bankruptcies in the paper. I may be one of them.

BILL: And that new addition Ralph and Sandy just put on the grocery store. I can see a huge mortgage and now fewer customers and poorer customers.

TAMI: You know who I worry about—it's Sophie. She always has lived so close to the edge. Always been so fragile. I worry about how she'll take this. Her job has been the one thing that held her together and got her up in the morning. I'd hate to see her do something stupid. We'd better keep an eye on her.

JOANNE: Gosh, are you ever right on that one.

BILL: Well, there's lots of others who are gonna need a bunch of cheering up and helping out.

GREG: So what do you say to someone like me who has worked at the plant all my life? That's all I know. I don't have any other skills. I'm a fish out of water.

BILL: So, who will sponsor the Little League? Well, maybe I should say, will there be enough kids for a Little League?

VICKI: I can't help but think of Shorty and Lucy having that exchange student come next month. They may be on welfare or unemployment by wintertime.

JOANNE: Yes, and what about Chuck Billings, just starting medical school at Stanford? Will he and his folks be able to swing that now?

BILL: There's gonna be a lot of people hurting. No question about it.

GREG: Even the truckers. Sounds like it won't take as many rigs to take concentrate as it did the juice. But they have a powerful union backing them. Still, they have families and bills to pay, too.

TAMI: Right, so who gains from all this?

VICKI: Who's the enemy? Who do I hate? I never did like Walt very much. Seemed like a kid with a degree in his hand, and he let you know he was just a little better than you. He won't be hurt. He'll just move on to the next plant. How can a city kid know about a little town? He doesn't know what it's all about.

BILL: You're right! You know he's just the messenger boy. He goes down to the latest meeting and they show him a bunch of graphs with the bottom line and then they tell him, "Now, go back and shut her down!" It's really no skin off his nose.

ROB: Yeah, when I wanted to punch him out at that meeting this morning, I said to myself, "What good would it do? He didn't do it." Guess he's just carrying out orders.

TAMI: But I wish he knew what it's like to walk in our shoes. Like you say, he'll just walk into another manager's job. Or he'll stay and take care of whoever's left.

VICKI: So, who cares? Does anybody care what's happening here? I really doubt it. That three-piece suit accountant who made the chart probably never missed a heartbeat. I can just hear it. "Gentlemen, this plant in Washington is just not cost effective. It's got to go."

BILL: I just hate those guys. What do they know about a day's work, getting sweaty and all. They drive from their air- conditioned condo in their air-conditioned Lexus to their air-conditioned office, wondering where they'll go for lunch today. I'd like to turn them over my knee and spank them.

VICKI: Ok, so I'll just shake my fist at all of them.

GREG: You know what I think of? Remember those ads during Vietnam when they showed the GI trudging along with the caption, "No Deposit, No Return"? I feel like that grunt! Everybody is just glad it's not them facing the music.

TAMI: Do you know what really bugs me? I was reading in the latest *Journal* that the board upped our CEO's salary to a seven-digit figure. I mean, with stocks and all it added up to that. So, he's basking in Puerto Vallarta while we wonder what's next. I ask you, what's wrong with this picture?

BILL: I saw that, too. Where is the fairness? Yeah, I know. I know. They'll all say that he'd just get hired away by some other big company and they need that salary to keep him. But I say, "Is anyone worth that much?"

JOANNE: When I know how hard we work, that just makes my blood boil! Now, wondering if we will even have that job gives me a mighty short fuse.

TAMI: I'm afraid we're a thing, a list of Social Security numbers on one of their tidy white sheets. Are we nothing but a commodity?

GREG: I think in the "Dilbert" cartoons we are human resources. Some euphemism, huh?

JOANNE: I guess they don't know about the land, either. Guess its just, what do they say, capital? But we love this place, we're people of the land. When I wake up in the morning, it's all that I see and breathe in and feel when I get my hands in the dirt. I don't think they get it.

VICKI: I still keep asking, "Who cares? Who do I scream at?"

BILL: I figure you can count on everybody dodging. The foreman, the manager, the regional guys, the CEO. They'll all duck the responsibility. Everybody's running scared. They have to do what they have to do. The bottom line rules and they have to bow down to it. No one has the guts to own up to what they did.

TAMI: Sure, they'll all say the stockholders forced them into it. If we don't show profits we'll lose their money. Can't you see the gray-haired folks in their Florida and Arizona retirement communities reading their dividend statements and calling their brokers to sell it off?

JOANNE: So are they the cause of all this? Those folks simply eager to make their next tee time or get back to shuffleboard? Are these folks our enemy?

ROB: Nah, I think they will say they just want the greatest return on their money, and they have nothing to do with our plant closing.

GREG: And the board will say that it's market competition and we have to stay competitive. Everybody's got some good reason so that it's not their fault. I want someone to 'fess up to what they're doing here.

TAMI: So it's probably the customer. That soccer mom who pushes her grocery cart down the aisle and chooses the cheapest cranberry juice on the shelf. Am I left with yelling at someone who looks a lot like me?

VICKI: I'm afraid my head is spinning. It's all pretty complicated. I live here because I want the simple life. What's so wrong with that?

TAMI: Sure, that's with all of us. That's why we stayed.

Six workers at the cranberry juice plant commiserate together at the Leeward Side Cafe after learning hours before that the juice line would close in less than two months. They were told that it was simply not cost-effective to make the juice near the bogs on the shores of Washington State and truck the product to Henderson, Nevada, the distribution center for the entire West Coast. The new plan would be to prepare a cranberry concentrate here to be transported to Nevada. Obviously, fewer trucks at lesser cost are needed this way. They were reassured that this change had nothing to do with their standards and quality of work and were told that there would be limited job opportunities in Henderson for persons willing to relocate. Since needless money was being spent daily, this change would be effective the first day of October.

At this moment the six friends are light-years away from thinking about forgiveness or even that forgiveness is something they should be considering. Rather, they are stunned. Their basic way of life is threatened; they are confused, hurt, and angry. The exasperation is that they have no known offender. Their talk is an effort to locate who threatens to take so much away from them. They are hardly successful. No one single person can be pointed out as the villain. Rather, they are dealing with one of a class of events in which the offender is an unquestioned value, a powerful idea, a firmly held belief, an accepted procedure, or a protected institution.

In this case the value is "profit," most often referred to today as "the bottom line" and the procedure is "restructuring" or "downsizing." Everything else is seen as less important or neglected. The chain of command bringing this unwanted news is composed of persons who embody that value or fear questioning it. No single person in the chain would be considered by most standards as bad or evil, just people trying to make a living, too. The workers express anger at what is placed as most important on the top of the corporate list and lament the discounting of so many other qualities that they value. They rightly feel "thinged."

In my opinion these invisible and far-reaching forces are more hurtful to more persons than any other today. Market forces, institutions, values, ideas, and traditions exert tremendous power over our lives and may with utter indifference hurl us into chaos.

This present story is an example of those powerful forces that now and in the past have shaped our lives in destructive ways: slavery, patriarchy, ethnocentrism, misogyny, war, prostitution, "the glass ceiling," female genital mutilation, child labor, colonialism, racism, classism, segregation, economic poverty, immigration quotas, servitude, marital inequality, totalitarianism, genocide, and voting polls. And the list may go on, with an accompanying list of those who have labored and suffered to loose the chains these distorted values have manacled persons with. The problem addressed here is how to forgive an idea, a value, an insitution, when so often the victims are left immobilized and defeated by an invisible hand. In the Western frontier the abused person could have it out with the abuser; no such oppportunity is available here. Any attempt to "duke it out" would end up in shadowboxing.

The results of these broken expectations of home, family, security, and community are much like those when we are harmed by an individual: shock, hurt, blame, anger, and vengeance. The greater difficulty is knowing where to place these feelings. An additional serious problem is the divisions that are created among groups of people, the soon-to-be-jobless and the employed, the unlucky and the lucky: the plant manager, the urban accountant, the regional office, the CEO, the board of directors, and the stockholders.

Let us consider the potential paths of forgiveness for these workers. The first is that in which they engaged so naturally, expressing their feelings intensely and fully. To even mention this pathway is laughable, as though these six persons could do otherwise. How could they meet on this occasion and talk about the weather, sports, and kids? They followed a well-known principle that emotions need to be expressed before rational thinking can emerge effectively. This way is much more healthy than the person who smolders within, leaves quietly fuming, and returns with weapons to wreak havok. Broken expectations and the consequences resulting need to be put into words wrapped in feelings. More quiet persons need to become aware of what they feel by hearing others speak their feelings. In many instances it is the women helping the men to do so.

It would be so neat and tidy if clearly defined steps were the process of forgiveness. Rather, it appears to be searching out one's way through difficult wandering. Intertwined with feelings is the equally important need to name the power acting upon them. I am tempted to say name the enemy, but that is not really true. Profit is the necessity of the free-enterprise system of capitalism and has produced many positive results in our nation and the world. The issue is more balance and harmony: profit harmonized with honoring nature, creating beauty, and building relationships. Naming what is happening allows proposing new and novel answers that may come far closer to meeting all needs in the situation. The workers are helped by knowing that cost-effective means are necessary to reach the valued corporate goal of profit.

Another naming process is knowing that when other values come into conflict with profit, they lose. Whether they are contracts, guarantees, promises, traditional practices, precedence, justice, fairness, family closeness, or community-mindedness, they lose. Such knowing dovetails with the assertion that there simply are no guarantees in our daily lives, save one. The blow is somewhat softened by knowing that anything can happen; life's road can make an unexpected sharp left turn. Not even searching for profit is a guarantee. In a coming generation another value may arise to take its place. But for now the greatest certainty is that action in accord with profit will be smiled upon.

Might other means be found than the one announced to them by the plant manager on that fateful morning? Experiencing feelings, naming the powerful value, and knowing that ultimately there are no guarantees may form the foundation for creating solutions.

A third pathway in this constellation of forgiving is addressing the compelling need to figure out what to do. To do nothing is to court disaster. Around this quest there will be sleepless nights and obsessed days. Again, it is unlikely that the workers would be able to avoid this task. It will simply be with them, even when they had planned on an enjoyable, peaceful summer. An unwelcome interruption came to their doors.

The more one is caught in the swirling confusion of not knowing the next step, the stronger will be those original feelings about being trapped in that whirlwind. In this arena of forgiveness, action centers more upon how to land on your feet, not working toward a reconciliation with the offender or attempting to empathize with him or her.

Thinking and acting as a group is often the path discovered by persons blown by the gale winds of powerful institutions. Something sacred and mysterious is found in the forming of community with others to face the winds. Certain experiences may occur when united with others that simply cannot emerge in one's individuality. Truly, any one of the workers might speak to the foreman or plant manager, either pleading a case to stay on or volunteering to go to the Nevada facility. The old adage that there is strength in numbers is true, but does not tell the whole story.

The workers' being in concert with one another opens the possibility of experiences that may lead to glimpses of a new vision of life itself. The workers may come to know for themselves the surprising richness of being in relationship in contrast to individually striving for increasing wealth. The vision of humanity as "person-in-community" may be contrasted with the traditional "economic man" [*sic.*] They may begin to feel the satisfaction of seeking the common good.

They might be gradually and largely unknowingly formed by the words of John Donne penned in the seventeenth century: "No man [*sic.*] is an Island, entire of itself; every man is a piece of the Continent, a part of the main. Any man's death diminishes me, because I am involved in Mankind; And therefore never send to know for whom the bell tolls, it tolls for thee."

Forgiveness is grounded and enriched by the knowing that our universe is totally interconnected. Whether we know it or not or like it or not, we are made up of relationships with all other entities everywhere. We affect and are affected by all happenings, not bouncing against the outside of us, but in the core of our being. Quality of relationships with all creation looms large as the highest value to be sought. Accepting and living in this new reality lessens the importance of guarantees and profit. Our individuality is always within the context of being equally embedded in community.

I am not implying that these six searching workers will have a religious conversion and live transformed lives thereafter; rather, from each of their present worldviews, they may well brush near this reality and feel its strength and wholeness. Thus, another segment of the path to forgiveness may well incorporate our unfailing connection with others, all others.

Let us look in on this same group again, now having lived with the grim reality for a time period and having talked a number of times during that time.

TAMI: I say we buy them out.

JOANNE: How in the world would we do that? We're not rich.

TAMI: Well, if we all took out home equity loans, we might come up with quite a bit. Our homes won't be worth much in a ghost town, so what do we have to lose?

BILL: Super idea. We wouldn't be the first to do it. You know United did it.

GREG: United?

BILL: Yeah, you know, United Airlines.

JOANNE: Like how much you put in means how many shares you own?

TAMI: I think so. It makes sense to me.

ROB: I'll have to think on that one.

VICKI: At least it's something positive. We've all been so down lately. We need to hear something good.

BILL: Well, I still think we need to find out what the union can do for us in this situation. I still haven't heard back from the steward, but she did say she'd look into it. Beats me what they might do, but I guess they've faced this in other towns besides ours.

TAMI: I'll sure be glad to hear when you find out something.

JOANNE: Well, several of us have been wondering if we could put out a new product. You know, like those specialty jellies or condiments that are packaged in fancy little jars and sold in gift shops and the big department stores. We've got some super cooks around here.

ROB: I would never have thought of that. Neat!

BILL: I know several people have gone over to Aberdeen to talk with the economic development office. They try to find industry to come into an area. They go courting, hoping they can win them here. Who knows who might be needing just what we have here?

ROB: You're sure right on that one.

VICKI: I know you all will laugh at this one, but I thought of it when I saw a magazine cover the other day. Do you realize that we live less than a hundred miles from two of the wealthiest people on earth—Bill Gates and Paul Allen?

BILL: You sure got that one right.

VICKI: All right, I'll start with the funny one first. Let's see if we could convince Paul Allen to bring the Seahawks here for fall and spring training camps. They always go over to eastern Washington and practice in the heat. Why not here in the mild weather?

JOANNE: I think you mean the rain!

GREG: Terrific sense of humor. Nice to hear a few laughs around again.

JOANNE: OK, let's hear the second one. I want to know if it's as good as the first one.

VICKI: This one is not tongue-in-cheek. Isn't there something we could do out here for Microsoft? I know that they have their Redmond campus, but I expect they don't want more people in cars adding to the Seattle area traffic gridlock. They just might like a satellite. Then in my more sober moments, I wondered of one of them would want to invest in our town. You know, they get something, we get something. After all they're both Washington boys who love what we've got here. Like, "hooray" for the little town!

TAMI: I'll applaud that one. Great thinking!

GREG: OK, since we're on a roll and we've all got our thinking caps on, let me try this one. The problem is transportation costs, right? Well, what if, instead of trying to buy the whole kit and caboodle, we get equity loans to buy a fleet of trucks? We run the finished product to Henderson ourselves. We keep our jobs and we lose some money on the trucking. We earn less, but we still have jobs and homes and a town.

JOANNE: Wow, that's good thinking. I'm glad you came up with that idea.

TAMI: It's so good I'd like to take it and give it a little twist. It's still with trucking. What if they continue to haul the juice to Nevada, and we all take a cut in pay equal to the percent it costs more to haul juice rather than concentrate? See what I mean? If it costs seven per cent more, we take a seven percent cut. Our salaries would be tied to the cost. You know, it would change from year to year. It's less, but we face losses whatever we do. After all, think of how much it will cost us to uproot and settle somewhere else. Or stay here and own property that's not worth anything.

ROB: I am really impressed with that idea. It speaks directly to what they are telling us is making our plant obsolete. So they keep the price down, we keep our community. We'll talk their bottom-line language.

JOANNE: I'm beginning to feel better listening to all your great ideas, but I'm still caught back on the two rich men. I don't know why we didn't think of this before. We are in the shadow of Boeing. How many times have we heard that as Boeing goes, so goes the rest of the state?

BILL: You're sure right on that one. I can remember a billboard in the sixties when Boeing was down. Remember? "Last one out of town turn out the lights."

TAMI: Yes, yes, how could we forget those times? Our son was one of those Boeing engineers who went to selling shoes. But go on with your idea.

JOANNE: We're closer to the main assembly plants than Wichita, Kansas.

We have a technical work force of people who have great work habits and a record of quality production. Couldn't we find a way to make some airplane part? After all, I hear with the big merger with McDonnell Douglas, parts will be made all over the country. We're so close and so good!

BILL: That is a really sound idea.

VICKI: We need people to get together and work out these ideas. Someone from economic development must know how to move them along.

TAMI: I guess I'm caught up in the present. We need to be ready to face some difficult months right away, not knowing if any of these ideas might materialize. I'm thinking of looking into unemployment compensation, seeing if the bank would accept only interest on our home loans for a while, and buying some food staples in quantity from the store. We may need to tighten our belts and work together 'til we see what's going to happen.

JOANNE: I fully agree. We need practical plans now.

BILL: I agree, too, but I've been wondering something the last few minutes. Maybe it's just a pipe dream and you'll laugh at it, but so what. What if we organized and sent a delegation to main headquarters with several plans? Maybe we just might help that CEO see that we both could win here. We keep our community; he has a reduction in costs. You know, talk his bottom-line language and share some down-home talk with him. Who knows? He might be a farm boy. He might even have a soft spot in his heart. Do you suppose he ever splashed barefooted through a mud puddle or caught a polywog in a slough? I suppose I'm willing to see if we can touch the human side of this man.

TAMI: I really like that idea. Maybe he needs to come here and see what we have here that doesn't show on the charts. I wonder if he has kids…and maybe a dog.

GREG: Sounds like a long shot, but what do we have to lose?

In their words we hear the formative beginnings of persons in community, affirming one another while searching for new answers for themselves and others. In the process through which they are moving they have avoided several important pitfalls. Forgiveness should offer us the joy of freedom, not be an entrapment. They did not remain focused upon looking back to the "good old days," wish they had been born a generation earlier, or continually lament their broken dreams. Nor did they remain stuck in the original feelings of anger, defeat, immobilization, or helplessness. They did not expend their energies repeatedly decrying the injustice or lashing out at one person, one group, one corporation, or one value. They were, rather, moving toward a new openness to their unique situation, one not faced by their parents or grandparents. They responded to the unique challenges of their day.

We do not know if anything will come of their endeavors. We leave them in ambiguity, at the formative beginnings. Yet the quality of their being together is in itself impressive and speaks of the end toward which forgiveness calls us. They may be on the brink of creating something new; but even if the worst happens, they will have the brief experience of community together. I am imagining One surrounding their conversation, holding them close, cherishing their every word, persuading the new, and encircling them with grace.

They may be joining the long line of splendor of persons who by social calamity and disruption were required to abruptly leave their vocations, lifestyles, and native lands. I think of the surnames that speak of long-abandoned vocations—the Smiths, the Cartwrights, the Millers—remnants of an earlier era that could not withstand the wave of the newly emerging forms.

I offer a personal word. This flight of imagination just completed was based upon an article in my local newspaper dated August 8, 1997. My search for an example of how to forgive an institution ended as I looked upon the sad faces of five women in their hard hats and hair nets listening to the news of their plant closing. I returned to that picture many times. As a boy who was raised on a sagebrush-bordered ranch at Roseworth, Idaho, and a rock-laden farm on the Snake River outside of Buhl, Idaho, and who visited the remains of his grandparents' store in the ghost town of Hamilton, Nevada, I shed tears for those in Markham, Washington. I salute you!

CO-CREATING WITH GOD

May I be aware of the presence of
    One who creates with us,
    who created yesterday,
    is creating now, and
    will create tomorrow.
May I cooperate with the Creative One,
    this mystery in our midst,
    opening myself to whom I may become,
    encouraging any blossoming in others,
    nurturing the flora and fauna,
    partnering with the soil,
    advocating for the earth.
May I live in awe of Your encircling presence,
    wondering at Your unending breadth,
    amazed by Your unmeasureable depth,
    held by Your all-encompassing web.
May I learn to gently set aside
    my strong need to be safe,
    my fear of taking a costly risk,
    my self-serving attitude to be right,
    my obsessive need to be in control,
    my self-limiting search to be approved,
    my unquenchable hunger to always know.
May I turn to catch a glimpse of Your vision, thereby
    cherishing the beauty that You persuade,
    fostering balance and harmony,
    living in the presence of contrast and variety,
    feeling the intensity of Your passion for life,
    trusting more in the times of tumult,
    speaking openly on behalf of grace,
    resisting all that would mar and deface,
    crying over the pain of any beloved,
    joining You in companioning all,
    thinking with a globe in my hand,
    honoring those who have gone before me,
    considering those who are yet to come,

sending good will to my enemy, Your friend,
searching for tasks You need accomplished.
May I listen for Your heart's desire for creation,
and know that as I seek after that,
two will be transformed,
myself and creation.

7

They Were Simply
Swept Away

The boys were putting the finishing touches on their log raft, a task they had worked on for two summers. A large rope secured two cross pieces to the pine tree on the shoreline, and two long poles allowed them to guide by pushing on the bank of the river. They could float downstream for a ways near the bank, then be stopped when the rope went taut. This design had proved to be great fun in their several trial runs.

Both sixth-graders, Brad and Rob were cousins, Brad living in the Seattle area and Rob in the countryside of the Columbia Basin. Their families had gathered at the lot by the Icicle River for many years. The property, situated several miles from the community of Leavenworth, served as a middle ground for meeting each summer. The beautiful, evergreen-laden mountains formed a perfect back-drop for the swiftly flowing river fed by the snow pack of the higher elevation. Both families pulled trailers to the site for their annual July gathering of the grandparents and the two families of the brothers. Both boys anticipated the time with relatives and each other.

When they considered the raft ready, the boys followed the well-established rules that an adult must be present to watch over their rafting. Since their fathers had left early that day to golf, their mothers agreed to watch, taking their recliner chairs and their newly refilled coffee cups to the small beach area that served as the launch site. It was a spectacular day, the sun high in the sky and the majestic mountain forming a mix of brightness and shade. Twice the boys floated the length of the rope with appropriate whooping and hollering accompanying their imaginary Tom Sawyer and Huckleberry Finn voyages.

The mothers were momentarily engrossed with the swimming of a younger brother and sister near the beach where they sat. Suddenly, laughter and yelling turned to splashing and frantic screams. A change in current had floated the loose rope, catching it onto the opposite side, so that when it pulled taut, the raft overturned; the boys lost their guide poles, and were thrown into the river. Brad grabbed onto the raft. Rob tried but was unable to find a grip. Brad screamed Rob's name as he watched him quickly disappear underwater and out of sight. Desperate to save his cousin, Brad let go, and he, too, entered the throes of the icy river. Emerging near the bank once, gasping for air, Brad was not seen again by the two mothers frantically racing toward the boys.

Black coldness seemed to swallow the two boys. Help arrived and massive searching, coordinated by the Chelan County Sheriff's Department, continued until nightfall. No sleep was had by anyone on the lot that night. Grieving and terror were punctuated by emergency telephone calls and headlights announcing the arrival of other family and close friends.

It was the next day when the bodies were found caught on some slightly submerged logs in a river bend some distance downstream from the accident. A July holiday turned to tragedy, an extended family was devastated, and two young lives were snuffed out.

It became the special task of four parents to face their untimely tragedy and to search for some measure of meaning in it. How they would come to terms with the unbearable loss was a long and difficult process, one that called upon the reservoir of their basic feeling for life and their religious beliefs.

Debra, Rob's mother, found comfort and relief in the idea that God had a plan for their son, and, even though they could not presently comprehend what that might be, she would accept and know that someday they would understand. Jason, her husband, could not join Debra in her explanation, since he lived by the understanding that God had originally created the universe and set in place natural laws. Violating them places you in deep trouble. He would speak no more about his son, the accident, or the deaths. For Jason, with jaw clenched, the issue was closed.

These meanings contrasted radically with the position of Chad and Bev, Brad's parents. They were angry, more accurately, enraged, by this loss. Given their great efforts to become pregnant, occurring only after several years of working with a fertility clinic, they simply could not agree with Jason or Debra. After all they had been through to bring Brad into this world, they simply could not believe that God could so quickly take him away.

Chad's rage brought him to the point of rejecting God outright. He would have no part of a God who could bring about miracles, then act in such a capricious way. The Bible was filled with the mighty acts of God, yet in their moment of dire need God appeared to be looking the other way. Bev struggled to maintain that some good would come from their tragedy. She believed strongly that God could do anything God willed to do—their pregnancy was a case in point—yet God did not will to save their hard-won and precious son. Bev could not bring herself to forgive God for somehow either allowing the deaths to occur or causing them to happen.

Bev's position brings us to the central concern of our story: the problem of the need to forgive God. Bev's conclusion is not unusual and usually appears when some form of natural disaster occurs. Often they are described as "freak accidents" or "acts of God." The class of events may well include the consequences of volcanic eruption, violent hurricane, fierce tornado, earthquake, tidal wave, flood, forest fire, avalanche, lightning storm, or torrential rain. Likewise, on occasions where the loss, injury, or death is not clearly caused by any person, including the victim, then there is reason to ask about God's role in the event. Unfortunately, God may be blamed and left unforgiven.

The problem may be posed in a contrasting way. Many speak of thanking God for performing a miracle on their behalf. If God can do miracles, and stories of miracles are told frequently, then why did not God enact a miracle on behalf of these two youths? Bev pondered this question in her heart and wondered if she would ever be able to forgive God.

To remain angry and not forgive God placed Bev in a double problem. She must deal with her grief over the loss of her son and now she must cope without her most powerful resource, her relationship with God. She has lost two intimate relationships.

For Bev the pathway to forgiveness is to reconsider her vision of God. Returning to my original vision, I affirmed that God is intimate, gracious, and persuasive. Bev allows us to consider the quality of the persuasiveness of God more fully. When one envisions God as influential, there is never a need to forgive God. Forgiving God centers around the image of God as almighty, powerful, and omnipotent. Since these images are so prominent in classical Christianity, it is no wonder that persons end up shaking their fists at the sky, screaming out at what God did or did not do.

I am saying just as emphatically that God was not absent during this tragedy, a contrast to what Jason believed. For him, God had created once, set the laws in motion, and watched from a distance the working of these laws. This picture is one of both unilateral power and uninvolvement, two basic differences with the vision I offer.

Debra's position would agree with Jason's in terms of the unilateral power of God, but differs as God is intimately involved with the lives of persons. For God to have a plan for Brad, mysterious and unknown, makes God more than persuasive and leaves Brad out of being influential himself.

I wish to be more specific about God as persuasive in the lives of people. Earlier I affirmed that the world is composed of the tiniest of events, the basic building blocks of the universe. Within each event several persuaders merge to create the next happening. The mix of influence will be different for each moment, but four ingredients will always be present: the world, one's body, one's past, and God's possibility. These important factors may be outlined to construct the final moments of Brad and Rob. The question addressed is: If God did not cause the deaths, allow the deaths to occur, or remain absent during the dying process, then how was God present?

We begin with the world. The accident could not have occurred without the presence of a natural environment, which in a sense contributed to the cause. There were surrounding rugged mountains, the result of cataclysmic events of the Ice Age, upon which snow accumulated during the winter months. The high temperatures of spring and summer melted the snowpack, forming tiny trickles of water, converging into ever-wider streams. There was a river flowing from mountain heights to lower plains, the carrier of the recently melted snow. The pine tree to which the rope was fastened and the pine poles used to construct the raft had evolved as one of the earliest forms of flora on our planet. All were components contributing to the unfolding events.

Internal combustion engines, steel and aluminum sheets forming the basic construction of the trailers, rubber tires to undergird both pickups and trailers, asphalt highways carved laboriously over the Cascade Mountains, and the natural fiber of the rope crafted by human technology were all part of the manufactured components of the world around the boys. The telephone and postal service provided the means by which family members coordinated dates and planned their supplies. Golf courses and golf clubs, immigrants from Scotland in our more recent history, allowed the two fathers to be away from the river that day. In the absence of any of these, the accident could not have occurred exactly as it did.

Samuel Clemens had given the world the character of Tom Sawyer over a century before, portraying the images that the boys had re-created. A raft was a necessary accessory to the role of Tom. The literary world formed a part of the backdrop for this accident.

While this may appear a strange way to explain the causes of the boys' accident, we are dealing here with an extremely complex and multifaceted event. Now we turn to a second area of influence, the boys' phyiscal bodies. Their bodies were a most intricate constellation of atoms, molecules, tissues, and organs organized into several intertwining systems. A youthful body exudes energy and seeks stimulation and novelty, follows the decisions of the will, provides significant information to the mentality, requires necessary conditions in order to function, and has definite needs for survival. The contributions of their bodies to this event were the striving for stimulation, the well-formed habits of physical balance and rapid responses, the energy to push, grasp, and swim, but also the limitations of even the most energetic body to massive water currents and hypothermia.

The boys also brought their past with them into this tragic moment. They remembered stimulating and challenging play on the river, the beginning of the raft last summer, the mistakes they had made in their earlier efforts, the improvements they had thought about through the school year, and the purchase of the longer, stronger rope. In more general terms, their past provided them with confidence gradually accumulated through many classroom and sports events. They knew that they could think well. Successes of their past taught them to expect success in the next venture, so they were confident and daring. Experiences in the wilderness area near the river gave them the wisdom to protect themselves. This same experience gave them respect for their parents' suggestions and requirements.

Most of the stage is set for the drama to unfold. All persuaders that will play a part in these moments are factors we may call the "what is" of the new moment. We are now ready to consider the "what might be" in the situation, possibilities offered by God.

Each moment as the boys were launching and riding the raft they were challenged by who they might become next. The actions they had already taken were now over and things of the past. God felt that moment with the boys and emerging from that feeling offered the new possibility of the next becoming. The first quality of every possibility is that it be the best action for both the boy and the entire creation. At times these whispers would be known by each boy, but more likely out of his awareness, felt perhaps as a slight nudge or little push in a new direction.

The second quality is that the possibility be appropriate and relevant for this next tiny event. Such tiny offerings stand in contrast to the usual way we consider God's having a plan for our lives.

The four important influences are in place. The curtain rises on the drama. The world is present in its majesty and fullness: towering mountain, blue sky, bright sun, fully running river, ice cold water, tall pine, log raft. The manufactured influences include primarily the thick rope and the scant clothing worn by the boys.

The boys bring with them well-rested and well-nourished bodies filled with energy and eager for stimulation. Their minds are sharp and alert, preparing for their launch. Their first two rides heighten the excitement felt through their bodies. God has offered the possibilities of thrusting their guiding poles, balancing well on the moving raft, attending to the multiple sensations of the ride, moving to caution as the rope neared its end.

The third launch brought with it a slight but deeply significant variation, as the rope floated under the raft and caught on a back crosspole. God's whisper of alertness and caution was met by the boys' increasing enjoyment and growing confidence. The boys were caught unaware, as they were not ready for the rope to end. They knew when to prepare for the lurch caused by the taut rope. What they did not know was that this time was different. Just as the rapidfire events occurred, so did the new possibilities from God come forth.

The possibilities offered changed drastically from enjoyment and stimulation to dramatic acts of survival. To surface, to see clearly, to reach, to grip, to paddle their legs, to scream for help, and to climb onto the raft were the likely calls to protection. As Rob lost his grip, probably due to the swift current and the shock of the cold water, Brad instantaneously plunged in after him. To what degree this was the call of a divine possibility, or more one of his own making, we will never know. The two mothers saw only the attempted rescue, but not the inner motivation.

Following that moment, the influence of the world was great. Two boys in the swift downward current of icy-cold water had little chance of survival. Even their fit bodies and their confident attitudes were no match for the natural persuaders. Divine possibilities of floating, breathing, keeping alert, reaching for overhanging bushes or half-submerged rocks, paddling toward the shoreside current were surely offered, yet met a youth increasingly unable to respond.

By stopping the action of this series of events, like viewing one frame of a moving picture, three tiny events might feature more clearly the participation of God and the other persuaders. I do not wish to sound presumptuous by assuming that I know specifically how God speaks to us; rather, I am taking literary license for the purpose of clarification. That I imagine God's purposes accurately is less important than that I show what makes up an event.

As they rode the raft for the first time that morning the world, the boys' pasts, their bodies, and God's possibility contributed positively to the outcome. For each of the boys God offered the goal of being keenly aware of all their senses. The world offered the best of a beautiful summer day, a gentle breeze, a cloudless sky, and a cooperating river current. It was certainly easy for the total being of the boys to drink in the beauty and feel the exhilaration of that brief span of time. Likewise, their bodies felt alive and tingling. All that influenced the outcome of that moment seemed to be in harmony and accord, creating a wondrous sense of intensity and wholeness. Persuaders did not conflict or offer radically contrasting possibilities for that moment of oneness.

The second tiny moment occurred during the third and disastrous ride on the raft. God beckoned Brad to look at the manner in which the rope was beginning to entangle with the back crosspole. At that very moment the world, in the form of Rob's voice, called Brad to look the opposite direction at a school of small minnows making their way downstream. Brad's body was a lesser persuader, willing to follow the direction of his decision to glance to the left. Brad's past was accustomed to respond to his cousin, so the well-founded habit was in place. In this event there was a clear conflict between persuaders, the one brought by the world being much more prominent than the one offered by God. The outcome was simply and innocently enough that Brad looked where Rob was pointing. Brad did not look at the entangling rope.

The third event is that brief moment after both boys were thrown into the water and Brad and Rob reached for the raft. Brad had a secure hold. This moment was Rob's. God's highest possibility for that moment was simply: Grip hard, hang on! Rob's past was in total agreement, for he knew the urgency of the moment and the necessity for him to save himself. However, Rob's body faced severe limitations in cooperating with the goal as it was experiencing shock, gasping for air, swallowing water, and being pulled downward. The world, likewise, presented the severe forces limiting his body, the icy-cold water and the swift downward undertow. A split was occurring as God's possibility and Rob's desire fought with the forces of the world and his rapid drain of body energy. God's possibilities were fully present, but did not prevail in that moment. Rob lost his grip and slipped into the water.

These imaginary events simply illustrate that God is only one of several powerful influences in each of our moments. At times those divine possibilities are actualized fully, unheard due to louder persuaders, or defeated by the more powerful influencers. My basic point is that God is present and persuading.

With this outline I affirm that God did not make the accident occur, did not simply allow the accident, and was not absent from the accident. Intimately present, blended with the other powerful persuaders creating those moments, God persuaded whatever was available to persuade, willing the best for the two boys and all creation. God was being who God is and doing that which God is able to do.

I cannot say that God is to be held accountable for the deaths of the boys and thereby stands in need of forgiveness. With this vision of God it appears to me that forgiveness does not fit and is not relevant.

My hope is that this vision would offer comfort to the parents of Brad and Rob. There is no question that the loss of a child is the most painful experience life can bring to us. These parents have enough grieving to endure that they do not need the additional problems of blaming, hating, or rejecting God. Quite the opposite, never in their lives would they ever be in greater need of the Graceful Presence. The tragedy, then, is that they could walk this tearful path alone, not being aware of the One who walks with them offering a lamp for their feet.

I wonder if raging against and blaming God may be the most debilitating of all the problems posed by being unforgiving. Earlier situations have illustrated that the emphasis on hatred, hurt, and vengeance deters us from hearing the whispers of God. We close ourselves off even more radically when we give up on God and cannot trust in God.

In a positive manner, the parents of the boys may be heartened by the presence of the persuasive God who was intimately involved with their sons and is now intimately present with them in their grieving and their laborious pathway toward healing. Such is my desire for Jason, Debra, Chad, Bev, and any parent who has suffered through a tragic and untimely loss.

Grace in All Creation

Creation is like a cluster of clouds,
  for in it we may see so many
  different forms and shapes.

The wisdom of our traditions
    tells us what to see,
    so that is what we do see.
The world surrounding us has
    so many names,
    so many faces.
The voices of our day tell us
    where we are going, and
    what is our destination.

Would that there were only
    one tradition,
    one voice.
For we are brought to a place
    to decide what we see in the clouds,
    and what we see surrounding us.
From the clamor of competing visions
    we must choose our own or
    decide not to choose.

Oh, for a mentor to show us
    how to make this awesome choice,
    and how to live out that choice.
On our choosing, creation stands silent,
    letting us name the cloud.
But we risk choosing wrongly.
Perhaps we should await
    more information,
    more maturity.

I choose grace!
In the midst of vast uncertainty,
    I choose grace.
The hills are alive with grace,
    and the seas proclaim grace,
    the mountains shout grace,
    the skies overarch us with grace,
    the birds sing of grace.

I name the cloud grace,
>   the stuff of the universe,
>   that which makes the world go 'round,
>   that which is closer than our breath.

All creation is imbued with grace,
>   for the Source of Grace is within all.
Whispering to be graceful to
>   brother and sister,
>   brother sun and sister moon,
>   brother wheat and sister grape,
>   brother stallion and sister lioness,
>   brother rock and sister stone,
>   brother stream and sister tree.
Whispering be graceful to all that exists,
>   luring us to be relatives
>   in an encompassing universal family.
Whispering to feel with the brother and sister,
>   gifting to the stream and the tree,
>   offering to the wheat and the grape,
>   sharing with the stallion and the lioness,
>   as we are gifted, so we give to our relatives.

Ah, but I would want more, much more,
>   but know that I do not need more.
I long for justice, peace, and fulfillment,
>   and work for their emergence out of ashes,
>   and grieve when my brother destroys my sister
>   and worry about the future of my wider family,
>   and have no certainty about my future
>   nor the destiny of all creation.
Some may say I am simply a fool, an idiot,
>   a hopeless romantic.
I do know that the four horsemen
>   continue to ravage the earth.
Brutality, starvation, and oppression
>   occupy much space in our world.

Competition, self-promotion, and individuality
  live within our corporate life.
Sexual abuse, domestic violence, and infidelity
  reside within our families.
Unfairness, greed, and nearsightedness
  are legislated in our marbled halls.
Poverty, disease, and racism
   pitch their tents in our rural areas.

Yet I sing of grace!
I decide for grace alone,
   that which cannot be taken from us,
   that which desires the richest for us,
   as for the total creation,
   that which accompanies us in every danger,
   and that which ultimately takes us home
   to Grace.
I do see it in the passing cloud.
I choose encircling grace!

8

Kids with Matches and Our Home Was Gone

Three boys set out to climb to Castlerock. The Saturday afternoon in September was warm as they walked the sloping, upward trail toward the bare rock that juts dramatically toward the sky. The hills around the valley were yellow and brown, a contrast with the white of winter and the pale green of spring. As they reached a plateau where the sloping hill meets with a steeper incline, they stopped for hot chocolate. Supplies were taken from the backpack, brush and grass were gathered for the fire, and the match was lit. The tinder caught on the third and last match. The cups were placed next to the fire as the boys anticipated their refreshments.

The gust of wind came when the boys were gazing down on the winding Columbia River below. By the time they looked back at their drinks the grass on the downward side of their scratched-out fire pit was smoldering. Frightened, the boys stomped on the burning grass and grabbed handfuls of dirt from the ground and threw it on the blaze. The flying soil appeared to fan the flames rather than smother them. The three cups of chocolate were thrown on the fast-moving flames. Nothing they tried stopped the widely expanding fire as it began its sweep down the hillside. Now frantic and totally helpless, the boys ran quickly down the other side of the incline as the flames, fanned by the afternoon breeze, raced down-ward with increasing billows of smoke belching skyward.

The worst fire the valley had known was in the making. Flames roared unchecked at a speed of eighty miles per hour toward the residential area nestled near the base of the hill. Those who might have seen the impending doom had precious little time to prepare. Homes nearest to the tinder-dry, grassy slopes caught fire first; then the torrent of sparks from one house inflamed the trees, bushes, or roof of the next home. The heat of the day, the tremendous speed of the flames, and the dryness of the homes and vegetation combined to form a surreal picture of one black, billowing smokepot after another.

Sirens rang out, fire trucks from miles around raced to the scene, police cars cordoned off the area to the growing number of curious drivers, homeowners frantically grabbed hoses to spray down their roofs, sprinkler systems were turned on to form wet, protective fences around their properties. Before the day ended, thirty-two homes were nothing but ashes. No human life was lost; however, several precious pets perished in the flames.

Toki and Rae owned one of those thirty-two homes. They had been doing their weekly shopping on that Saturday afternoon and had been enjoying lunch out. During their lunch they had com-mented on the number of shrill sirens disturbing that pleasant fall afternoon. Upon leaving the restaurant, they first saw the hazy smoke that gave the sun a strange reddish appearance. As they crossed the Columbia River bridge, they were stunned to see the location of black, billowing smoke.

It was their neighborhood. The closer they drove, the more traf-fic they encountered, frustrating their desire to get home quickly. As they were still blocks away, a police car sat blocking the street, red lights flashing. The officer was directing people away. When Toki spoke to the officer he learned that he would have to show his driver's license to verify that he was from the cordoned neighbor-hood. They were told that they could proceed to the next neigh-borhood, still a safe distance from the frightening blaze. They parked and walked to the nearest view point. Through the thick smoke they could see that where once had stood a row of homes, nothing was left except the decimated remains. All that they owned were the clothes they wore and the car they drove. They learned from several equally stunned neighbors that it was too dangerous for them to even enter their street. Police would guard the area until enough cooling had occurred for persons to rake through the ashes for any remaining valuables.

Tuesday morning found Toki and Rae standing before their lot. Both knew that Miki was somewhere, cremated in the thick white ashes and the blackened remnants. A member of their family during their entire married life, their precious cat was now gone. With a stick Rae began to poke and prod in the various rooms of what was her home. Each room brought increasing disbelief and uncontrollable bursts of tears. The flower print hung over the fireplace, the antique clock that sat on the mantel, the comfortable chair that had belonged to Toki's father, the piano that Rae had saved for so diligently to purchase, the buffet in the living room filled with the china dishes from several generations, the linen tablecloths and napkins that had been a wedding gift to her grandmother, the set of cooking pans that hung on hooks over their kitchen stove, the file of recipes that Rae had loved to collect over the years, the address book of family and friends kept at Rae's small corner desk, the beautiful plants that Toki nurtured so carefully in their breakfast nook, all now were destroyed or forged into gnarled bits of metal.

Silence accompanied them as they slowly walked in the ashes and embers. So much was gone, so much of their heritage totally lost. On the practical side, the business records of receipts, bills, and checks, and on the side of aesthetics, the many books lovingly collected over the years. The closet off the family room was where the photo albums and Christmas decorations were stored, both links with the past now broken. Pain accompanied the awareness of their loss. Rae remembered her wedding dress, carefully stored in another closet. Disbelief returned as they recalled their clothes, each item with its own story of when and where it was purchased and its accompanying pieces that made up their favorite outfits. Replacing them seemed an overwhelming task. Toki and Rae pondered the moments it took to destroy that which they had taken years to acquire. It seemed like amnesia in which they had lost their entire past.

They learned from their neighbors how the fire had started, although the authorities were not releasing the names of the boys because they were minors. Anger emerged! Thoughts ran amok.

"How stupid!" "Dumb!" "Didn't they know better?" "Why didn't they use their heads?" "They didn't think and we lost everything!" They gave lectures to one another on what was happening to this generation of young people. They fervently wished the boys had known better.

Vengeance rushed forward with images of smashing their bikes or skateboards, ripping up their favorite NFL shirts, burning the autographed pictures of their favorite NBA players, and crumpling their school class pictures. In this way they would know how it felt to lose everything, especially the precious belongings.

Anger turned to other means of wanting the boys to suffer. Bringing a legal suit against the families would surely do that job, but whatever they won in court, the financial gain would be a mere pittance in comparison with the staggering losses of the thirty-two families. Anger and vengeance brought forth many scenarios meant to strike back and perhaps soothe the gaping losses. But even this avenue could not in any measure bring back those irreplaceable, precious belongings. There had to be a better way and, in their better moments, they considered those options.

In spite of the mix of feeling that swirled through their consciousnesses, Toki and Rae began the tedious and detailed tasks of gradually rebuilding their home and their lives, first from their motel room, and later their rented apartment. They would frequently remark that they now had a new feeling for what the history books they had read so lightly called warfare, refugees, and emigration.

Toki and Rae were greatly helped by having each other, a person with whom to sift through the ashes and to gradually watch the Phoenix arise. Their relationship with each other was intact; their relationships with precious objects that gave their lives meaning and beauty were void.

This story is one in a class of events in which, due to another's actions, precious belongings are damaged or destroyed. Usually those losses are spoken of as loss of property, although such a description hardly captures the feelings we invest in that with which we surround ourselves. A favorite car may be totaled by another driver's accidental loss of control, an engagement ring may be mistakenly mixed up with another ring at the jewelers, a front window and special vase may be broken by a misthrown ball, the newly laid living room carpet may be stained by a guest spilling red punch, unique houseplants may be irreversibly stunted by the lack of watering from a friend caring for them.

A key factor in this class of events is that the offender has no intention to do harm, allowing the pathway to forgiveness to be easier than if injury were the goal.

If any phase of the story of Toki and Rae is important, it is that forgiveness must begin with facing fully and feeling fully the loss of relationships. Implicit in this story is the assertion that we are made up of our relationships; they are central, real, and deep. Witness a friend losing a well-loved pet or a long-cherished pen.

Admittedly, in the earliest moments of the tragedy, denial and disbelief is totally natural. To take in the mammoth loss in one moment may bring the person down, prompting a loss of consiousness from the massive flood of unwanted reality. This phrase is often cried out, "I cannot believe that this is happening to me." Still, acceptance of the blend of feelings accompanying the tragedy is crucial for proper healing.

Here we meet again the results of injustice and unfairness, second cousins to having given rights that persons deserve. Toki and Rae would surely believe that with all the care and precautions taken, they would have the right to a safe haven at the end of the day. That right appeared to them not too much to ask of life. They earned it fairly, were paying for it through hard work, and were being responsible citizens and neighbors; thus they were due certain benefits. Again, all this is true but not totally comprehensive. The total picture tells us that we have no guarantees, as history reveals all too starkly. But grace offered through the graceful One is guaranteed, such that there are three sifting through the ashes. This same grace accompanied our forebears in their losses of native lands, homes, and possessions. It may seem as though innumberable cycles are experienced before the reality of grace alone emerges. The companion whispers for those who have endured losses to accept the present condition, however painful, and search for new possibilities to be found in the new stark reality.

Since Toki and Rae had not been in relationship with the three boys, the path of reconciling appeared irrelevant. The boys were from another neighborhood that had not been inflamed. Authorities who dealt with them were clear that to require that the boys face the victims would serve no purpose other than to traumatize them again. The original trauma was enough. Consequences set by the court in conjunction with the parents largely required volunteer service and fire safety classes.

Empathy was a possible path to follow. By recalling what they had done in their youth, they could build relationships of understanding. They knew that they, too, had made mistakes and errors of judgment. Not with such serious consequences as these, but nonetheless, damage was inflicted upon others. Toki had lost control of his father's new convertible and it had been totaled; Rae had, with the intention of helping her mother, ruined the surface of her mother's grand piano by using the wrong polish. Yes, they had made their share of youthful mistakes. They, too, were scolded with, "Why didn't you think?" Seeing the boys in a new light by seeing their own youth in them offered increasing degrees of healing for them. Nonetheless, when decorating for Christmas or imagining which outfit to wear to a reception, the starkly vivid losses rushed them through the entire range of feelings again. Their hope lay in moving through the cycle faster and with less intensity, not that they would never experience it again.

The path of forgiveness here is to hold gently to the possessions we own, knowing that we have no ultimate right to them and that they may evaporate before our very eyes; to hold tightly to the relationship with the Graceful One who is totally trustworthy and steadfast; to feel with all its force the pain of loss rather than attempt to avoid the hurt; to enter the world of the offenders to search out the common humanity shared with them; and to accept the recurring cycle of the swirling feelings.

Intention is crucial in forgiveness. What if the three youths intended to harm? We face, then, a much different situation. Let us turn the kaleidoscope slightly so that we create a different picture—three boys whose motivations were not a pleasurable climb on a warm day, but whose desires were to destroy a home.

Toki and Rae return from a weekend away. Entering the driveway, Toki first notices that something is awry when his garage door opener does not work. He attributes the problem to a battery and walks to the front door. There he is met with a cataclysm! All his senses register alarm. He turns and calls for Rae, who can hear in

Toki's voice that something is deeply wrong. They hang onto one another as they reel from the sight before them. Their home has been trashed!

Graffiti is scrawled on the walls with paint from the garage. Ashes and blackened walls tell of a large fire in the fireplace. Broken and shattered china is strewn across the dining room. Holes have been punched into walls with a hammer. Dirty dishes and half-finished food clutter the breakfast nook table. The refrigerator door is open, revealing spoiling food. Videos are smashed—their celluloid tapes strung and entangled throughout the family room. Books are ripped in two or half-burned in the fireplace. The television monitor is shattered, leaving glass scattered in the family room. The VCR is ripped from its wires and lies in the corner. Clothes in the closet are torn and strewn randomly. Medicines float in the unflushed toilet bowl. The disheveled bed is stained and gives off the stench of urine. Mikki lies dead in the litter box with her body burned and a plastic bag over her head.

The third match must have been used in the guest room, for there lay newspapers, torn books, and an empty book of matches over a charred section of carpet. It appeared to Toki and Rae that the parting shot was to torch the house had the fuel caught on fire.

After the initial shock they punched in the numbers 911 to reach the police. It was then they learned that the telephone wire had been cut. The trashing did seem to be complete. With the neighbors' help, the authorities were called, and they set about the necessary steps to file a report. Friends helped them to put some order into the chaos of their home so that they might at least sleep there before they both went to work the following day.

Toki and Rae were aghast, thrown into total shock. It all seemed so senseless, acts of wanton destruction. They could not understand this violence. Why? Why? Why? To their own question they had no meaningful answer. When asked by investigators for any possible suspects, the couple were speechless. They had no known enemies, nor did they suspect any individuals who might be seeking some type of revenge. The acts remained an utter mystery to them, leaving them to fear that the criminals might return.

Protection is surely in order for Toki and Rae, to be fostered by requesting police surveillance, changing their outdoor locks, and installing an alarm system. Protection would be greatly enhanced by having the violators apprehended, charged, and convicted. Rage appears the most appropriate feeling in their situation. Many words were spoken about what they would do if they caught the culprits, knowing that their being apprehended later was highly unlikely. Their anger is of a different order than in the first scenario. The obvious motivation to harm, epitomized by the torture and death of their cat, led to more intensity in response.

The pathway open to them here is to express their appropriate rage, their utter mystification; then, while in a mode of protection, grieve their awesome losses. But they would find it nearly impossible to enter the world of the violators. They could find little in their own experiences comparable to the magnitude of this destruction. Of course, they could recall moments of desiring to destroy something, but this was beyond their imagination.

They would search for and share theories about the intent of the destruction. They could not keep from longing to make sense of acts so painful to them. Was it an initiation for a gang? Were they proving something to someone else? Was it a weekend drug party that got out of hand? Were these youth so filled with rage that any target would do? Did they have some unknown grudge against the homeowners? Was it prompted by the thrill of some dare? Were they homeless from the riverfront? Was it a thwarted robbery turned to destruction? Was it a weekend hideout for several runaways?

It seems highly unlikely that their questions will ever be adequately answered, unless the youth are apprehended and one bargains to testify against the others. Even then, believing the testimony may be risky unless there is a trail of such destruction to verify the words. All in all, Toki and Rae may have to walk the path of forgiveness without knowing the motivations involved and without being able to to try to empathize with the destroyers. This is a more difficult path than if they could feel some common humanity with the boys.

Accepting their losses, refurbishing their home, maintaining that protection which is possible, and remaining open to life without massive cynicism and bitterness may be a likely path.

Another realization to accompany their steps is to know that in our fully interconnected world there are those who are radically destructive and deeply enraged persons, both endowed by heredity with certain character structures and taught by irrational physical abuse in early life. They are among us. We cannot predict when or where they will strike, snuffing out life or violating precious property. Their presence is one reason, among a number of others, that rights are precarious and vulnerable, for rights have no meaning to such persons. Our task is to protect ourselves to the degree we are able, while praying for these distorted persons in the same manner we pray for ourselves: that they will gradually open to the possibilities of transformation offered by the the One who loves them, us, and all life. It appears likely that to enter into such a prayerful attitude may well take years beyond this destructive assault. As Toki and Rae foster an openness to Grace in their lives, so they may be open to the well-being of those who harmed them. Echoing here is the challenge: Love your enemies.

As in the courtroom, so in forgiveness, motive is important. The path to forgiveness veers in a different direction depending upon the intention of the offender. Yet there is a common journey that both roads follow, the necessity of naming and grieving the losses.

A Litany of Loss

I cannot believe my own eyes.
I must be having a nightmare,
    from which I will soon awaken.
But I have already pinched myself.
I have no memories to help me here,
    nothing with which to compare it.
So much that I loved is gone!
Not as before when I lost a special pen,
    broke a cherished vase,
      or damaged my valued car.
I keep wanting to not believe
    what is obviously before me.
Someone whom I do not know
    or something I do not control
      has taken it all away.

I am sickened in my stomach!
I am enraged and see red!
I am hurt beyond words!
My heart is breaking!
  I cry unstoppable tears!
  I am filled with revenge!
I am swirling in confusion!
I am unsure if I can go on!
I have been destroyed, violated, raped,
  and I long to lash back and destroy.
I am tensed and agitated,
  ready to act,
  but no action comes clear.
At least I may count my losses,
  facing them one by one.

There are those unique relationships
  with my childhood that cannot be replaced:
  my family photo album,
  my baby book,
  my favorite adventure book,
  my tattered but loved doll,
  my first Bible,
  my earliest diary,
  my grade school class photographs.
I bid each of them a tender farewell.
Goodbye, dear friends…Goodbye!

There are those severed relationships
  with which I must deal now.
Those that took years to form
  must be must replaced quickly:
  new dining table and chairs,
  bedroom set and dressers,
  living room sofa and chairs,
  refrigerator and stove.
Energy and time are given,
  reluctant simply to do again
  what was done gradually before.

But relationships with the institutions
    that surround my life must be
    placed in order once again.
Tax records, current bills,
    unanswered letters, addresses,
    mortgages and contracts.
Telephone calls, letters, appointments
    fill my day and sap my energy.
    I feel the resentment of requirements,
    that I do now that which is
    required of me.
I am blocked from doing those
    exciting and creative tasks
    that earlier were beckoning me.
I lament the loss of my choice of
    employing my time and energy
    as I would choose.
I recognize that the theft of those
    precious commodities,
    once gone, do not return.
I bid farewell to my precious
    time and energy.

There are those relationships that
    surrounded my daily living with
    beauty, pleasure, and enjoyment:
    my loving pet,
    an original signed painting,
    my favorite recliner chair,
    the carved statue of Saint Francis,
    the sculpture of The Thinker,
    my mother's turn-of-the-century piano,
    a collection of favorite sheet music,
    tapes and disks of Broadway favorites,
    shelves of carefully selected books,
    china dishes displayed behind glass,
    the antique cherry wood secretary.

I know that I will unknowingly look for you,
    expecting that you will be
    where you have always been.
I know that I will feel a surprising sadness
    as I see not you, but a void.
I know that I will once again find myself
    swirling through all those feelings.
Yet I must thank you for the time
    we had together.
Rejoice in the pleasure experienced
    in our relationship.
And let you go…

No, I cannot…
Yes, I must let you go…
But I am heartened
    for you were not an object out there
    now completely gone
    but a relationship with me
    composing who I have been
    and now fully present in my memory.
I am reminded that every event
    filled with rich relationships
    is gathered up and saved
    in the life of grace.

9

I Just Can't Live
with Myself

It had been a great day at the lake. A cloudless sky, the temperature in the eighties, and a glassy smooth surface made perfect conditions for water skiing. The family had gathered at their lake cottage for the weekend, and now Sunday night was upon them. Rather than stay overnight and leave early the next morning for work, Ray and Bill decided to drive home that night.

They said their farewells, climbed into Ray's sports utility vehicle, and began their hour-long trip south. The darkness punctuated by the rare oncoming headlights, the rhythmic beat of the rock radio station, the humming of the powerful engine, and the reflection of the moon in the river winding next to the road combined with the results of an active day in the sun to give a hypnotic effect to the young men. As they approached the dam, signaling that they were about seven miles from home, Ray dozed off momentarily.

On a slight curve his car veered across the center line, placing them directly in the path of an oncoming van. Jarred from his brief loss of awareness by the bright headlights shining in his face, Ray desperately pounded his foot on the brake and wrenched the steering wheel to the right. The effort was too late. The two vehicles smashed head-on. Ray's vehicle spun to the right, back-end first, ending up on the side of the road. The van flipped on its side and was instantly consumed in flames.

By the time the emergency vehicles arrived, Ray and Bill had pried open the passenger side door and were frantically and helplessly watching the carnage of seven people burning before them on the highway. All died at the scene, a family and two friends returning home from a holiday trip. Ray and Bill were taken by ambulance to the regional hospital for treatment, although their shock rendered them nearly unaware of their physical injuries.

Awakening from the strong sedative the next morning and running his hand on the cool metal guards of the hospital bed, Ray gradually focused upon his father sitting next to him. His head and chest hurt, and when he tried to reach out, he found that he was limited by an IV in his hand. Taking a few moments to gather his senses, he asked, "Dad, where is Bill? What happened to those people? All they told me last night is that they would have a report this morning." His father told him the grim news of the fatalities. Ray burst into tears. From the other side of the bed, his mother moved near and embraced her sobbing son.

Ray learned that Bill would be released from the hospital the next day, after twenty-four hours of observation. Ray was fortunate in that his injuries were slight. Later in the morning the state patrolman came to verify information that he had taken from the hysterical young men the night before. Ray would probably face legal charges. He felt a cold sweat form over his entire body, and his stomach became nauseated. Suddenly, in the blink of an eye, Ray's life had changed from that of a happy, carefree young adult to a man facing stern consequences both within and without.

As the days passed, Ray healed physically, but sleep eluded his efforts. Daytime brought flashbacks of the searing headlights, the screeching crash, and the dying family. Peace was not to be had. Each reliving of the scene would be followed by a redoing of his actions. This time he would do it right. He would stay overnight and drive when fresh and alert. He would rest before the trip home. He would open the car window to allow the rushing air to keep him awake. He would stop at the little minimart for a break and a drink. He would ask Bill to spell him at the wheel when halfway home. He would see the van sooner and return to his lane. He would grab for the steering wheel faster.

In those rare moments of sleep, he would awaken screaming and reaching out desperately with both arms. The repeated redoings sapped his energy.

Try as he might, he was totally unable to get the family off his mind. The newspaper carried a story about the accident. He read each family member's name from the obituary. He learned that he would still be hospitalized during the funeral services. With great hesitancy and utmost difficulty, he haltingly composed the most difficult letter of his life, simply addressed to the friends and wider family. He later read the article describing the mass funeral held in the local Catholic church. Ray continued to be haunted by their deaths. What could he do? How could he ever make it up to those left behind? He found no fully satisfying answers to these burning questions. Remorse, guilt, and regret filled Ray's days.

As if these struggles were not enough, Ray felt the eyes of the community burning into him. He just knew that they would see him as some irresponsible dopehead leaving one more tragedy in his wake. He knew that was not true, but how would they ever know? How could he face others as he went to work and dealt with customers?

To allay the heavy guilt, Ray tried to shed the responsibility by placing it upon another. Why didn't the other driver hit his horn? Why in the world were so many people jammed into one car? Wasn't it rather stupid to be driving the last lap of a long trip so late at night? Why didn't he brake down sooner? This venture proved fruitless, for with each accusing question, Ray had to conclude that the driver had no fault. He was simply driving his family home from a holiday responsibly keeping in his own lane.

His biggest enemy, as with so many of us, was himself. From within he heard the sharpest criticisms and castigations: Careless...self-centered...irresponsible...stupid...unforgivable...inept...impulsive... hurtful...unthinking...foolish...! An unending flow of words were spoken by the voices that had the greatest impact on him and which could readily drown out any more comforting or reasoned voice from outside.

In his more lucid moments Ray realized that he would never be the same again. He was responsible for the deaths of seven people: Yes, the fiery death of an entire family and two of their friends. His innocence was behind him. A few seconds had radically changed his life and ended their lives. He had heard veterans speak of combat causing the loss of innocence for them, and now he knew of it in his own experience.

He decided to spend a few days with his married sister on the coast to see if that might help him to feel better. She and her husband were very understanding, but when darkness fell and he placed his head on the pillow all the familiar ghosts came to haunt him. Would anyone speak for him? But then, how could they, when he had done such a terrible act? He deserved everything he got. It was while away that he concluded that he simply could not live with himself.

Our story allows us to consider the subject of self-forgiveness, one of our most difficult tasks. More specifically we will address the unique pathways that lead to forgiveness. This scenario illustrates a class of issues in which persons suffer the aftermath of having harmed another: betrayed, physically injured, embarrassed, used, lied, broken promises, neglected, or embezzled. The offense may be relatively minor or deadly serious, apologized for or left unresolved. As with Ray, the scene is usually replayed repeatedly in the daily life of the offender, invading both the present moment and restful sleep. Life can become an unbearable, living hell.

The first step on the path is to talk with another person. Ray needs to talk though the tragedy, slowly describing as completely and as clearly as possible each event that occurred. Each particular picture needs to be painted with the accompanying feelings experienced and the ideas thought in that moment. Of special importance is to speak out any decisions that he made about himself in those shocking events. What did Ray see, feel, smell, hear, taste immediately before the crash, as they frantically pushed the door open, as he witnessed the burning van, when he realized there was nothing he could do, when the patrolman and other travelers arrived on the scene, when he was treated by the medics, when he was lying on the gurney in the ambulance, and when he was lifted into his hospital bed prior to the sedative?

Did Ray make powerful decisions? "My life is over. I don't deserve to live. I need to be punished for this. I should have died with those poor people. I'll never forgive myself for this. I'll never live this down. I'm a loser, complete loser." Once decided within, they can   easily be forgotten, yet guide from his depths the living of his days.

The experiences need to be put into words as the listener reflects in words what is being heard. To leave cataclysm and tragedy unspoken and unnamed grants it massive power over the person. Words spoken and words heard give us more awareness and ultimately more control. Interestingly, the listening process is a reflection of that empathic understanding that God offers to us in every event. Ray would be helped to know that there is One who lovingly felt with him, and with everyone, in each of those tragically unfolding moments.

Ray had already begun an important step on the path toward forgiving himself when he gave up the attempt to place responsibility for the accident upon someone other than himself. To heal, one must honestly acknowledge what he or she did or did not do. Ray did doze off. He, who was in control of the vehicle, did not carry out his responsibility. His lapse of awareness was the primary cause of the accident, radically closing down the other driver's options. Tragically, he caused the deaths of seven people and the injuries sustained by his friend and himself. He did those acts, for which he stands fully accountable and responsible. However, he is not responsible for intending to cause the tragedy. Talking clarifies his responsibility, just as it places realistic limits on his responsibility.

Bringing forth the ideas thought and the decisions made allows for some degree of discrimination between the actual events that occurred and the overlay of meaning given by Ray to those events. It is well known that the meaning given is often vastly different from the happening. He may have already condemned himself and begun his own punishment, serving as his own judge and jury.

Courtroom language brings us to another segment of the path to forgiveness. Ray needs to face whatever action the justice system takes with him on behalf of the deceased or the state itself. Reaching forgiveness is facilitated by being responsible to the wider community, for they, too, were offended by Ray's action. Whatever sentence is mandated by the court is to be accepted as a means of reparation for the offense, addressing Ray's earlier question of how he could ever make this up to them. Of course, abiding by the sentence is simply a symbolic gesture, never replacing the precious lives that were lost. God, while persuasively present with every person, cannot protect Ray from the consequences that are brought about by the decisions of the offended people or the events of nature. Ray must face them with the companionship of God's caring presence.

A central task in Ray's struggle toward forgiveness is to cope with his own inner committee in contrast to the many public settings he will face. Those inner voices, many of which he has already heard, may well be the most critical he will hear anywhere. When any proposal is made by Ray it must be convincing to the jury within. Shall he require himself to complete some penance? Will he meet the terms of the inner committee for accepting himself? Is forgiveness of himself an option at all? Must he live the rest of his days with condemnation felt from inside out?

Just as juries wrestling with a verdict wrangle and argue, so will the varied and complex voices within Ray. He will undoubtedly wonder if there is any hope of bringing balance and harmony to his own inner gathering. Some had already spoken the most critical and damaging words against him. Each voice needs to be given a fair hearing and encouraged to speak as critically as it wishes, to demand what it would have Ray do, and to explain the purpose those actions would accomplish. Surprisingly, even the most caustic voices, if queried carefully, usually do not have the ultimate goal of punishing or destroying Ray. The critical voice often masks its higher purpose, such as wanting Ray to carry out tasks with excellence, be appropriately cautious, or consider the needs of others. Yet they are often expressed in the well-known imperatives: "Don't... You'd better not... Stop it... Think, boy, think!" They are not to be silenced by force, for they will simply return another day. Rather, they are to be respected for the wisdom and value they bring to the aftermath of this tragedy.

Each of these voices is associated with the person Ray was during earlier stages of his growing-up process. They are not the unreal voices of a hopelessly deluded person. The complexity of our being human means having voices from our past, some helpful, other harmful, but all relevant at an earlier phase of our lives. Being able to name them as real persons, as well as to recognize their familiar messages, is greatly helpful to Ray's process of self-forgiveness. Surely, some will remain hidden and mysterious, without a name, known only by a familiar feeling or sensing. Ray will know them simply by not feeling right about some act he is considering or, conversely, by knowing just that something is true. No rhyme or reason supports these sensings, knowings, intuitions—they are just so.

Let us imagine the outer voices that were taken into him and made his own. His mother speaks repeatedly to the toddler, "Be careful!" His fathers tells him, "You can do it, come on, you can do it!" The tee-ball coach keeps urging him, "Keep your eye on the ball." Teammates yell to him in right field after he just misses a fly ball, "Flick it off, Ray, flick it off!" His shop instructor repeatedly lectures, "Measure twice, cut once." The literature teacher frequently paraphrases a famous poem, "I took the road less travelled and that made all the difference." His grandfather advises him, "If you're going to do a job, do it right."

As Ray has gradually made these many messages his own, they take on his voice, as well as theirs. They sing a duet. Some are definite requirements that he make all the right moves, whereas others are understanding about mistakes made. Within Ray at this time the rightness voices outnumber the gentle voices. The critical voices from within are usually much more outspoken and much more readily identified.

Further listening is usually necessary to hear the comforting, soothing, and nurturing voices or those who speak with a more measured and reasoned tone. Conversations among the more comforting and the more critical voices may begin to restore a much-needed balance to the new ideas yet to come. It is not difficult to imagine the mixed reception given by his inner committee to this proposal: I will accept myself and what I did. At the moment it would seem unlikely that this legislation would be passed, this proposition would win over the jury, this suggestion would be approved by the committee. The "do it right" votes outnumber the "give yourself a break" votes. Often, through dialogue, the voices learn that they have many goals for Ray in common. Doing things right and being kindly to oneself may be only contrasting needs of the desire for Ray's well-being.

In the midst of this process of proposing and deciding, a form of inner conversation, the voice of God can be of ultimate significance. If Ray has no faith, nor any relationship with God, or a belief in a fully righteous and just God, his efforts at self-forgiveness will be much more difficult, perhaps impossible. However, if within this inner gathering of voices there is the voice of grace, then surely forgiveness will come. The message of grace in this situation will be that which creates the best for this guilt-ridden young man and all parties affected. No words of punishment or condemnation will be uttered. Rather, the lure will be as it has always been: Given these circumstances, who will you become next?

God will also know the totality of voices gathered, for grace was persuading and influencing their births and development. Even the hidden and mysterious are known to the Intimate One who knows and loves all creation, including all of the intricate parts of Ray. In the difficult pathway Ray is treading there will be a powerful affirming voice advocating for his well-being and continued blossoming. Grace will speak regardless of Ray's faith stance; he need not know it is happening for it to happen; however, the power of grace increases dramatically if Ray does know God's presence. It might sound something like this: I know that parts of me want to chide me, punish me, condemn me, call me hopeless, but there is One who approves of me regardless of my past.

One segment of the path toward self-forgiveness, then, is the necessity of dealing with oneself in his total complexity and variety. To know the presence of the intimate, persuasive, and gracious is of utmost importance in traversing that rocky, upward, winding way.

Thus far the pathway has included speaking truthfully to oneself and to another about what one did and did not do, accepting the responsibility for both, being willing to accept the consequences, and struggling with the inner voices regarding acceptance. We turn now to a new question primarily focused on the relationship of Ray with God: Will God forgive Ray? Thereby, may Ray be free to forgive himself?

Traditionally it seems we speak as though God either turns away in anger when we do something wrong or God, who is already apart, chooses no longer to draw near to us. Separation is the net result in either. In the vision that I offer, God is simply never distant. Whatever we do or don't do, God remains intimate with us. Let us review the particular form this closeness takes.

I return to the primary ways that God relates to us in any given moment. God feels fully with us what has happened in the just-completed moment and from the depth of that empathic understanding offers a possibility both relevant and enriching for the next. Following the particular choice made by the person from the many possibilities vying to be fulfilled, including God's, God saves that actuality in God's own life everlastingly. God empathizes, persuades, and saves. There is no coming and going, no drawing near and separating afar, no angry withdrawal in this vision. God may be fully trusted to be present always to offer a possibility of who we may become next.

Perhaps now we may be able to fit together the traditional and the newer way of envisioning God. In the new vision, God forgives us in each new split second; that is, God is present with a lure lovingly offered that is the most enriching possibility both for us and for all creation. It appears to me that the desired result that is requested in tradition, a togetherness, is simply assumed to be present in the new. Put another way, in the new vision, we need not ask for what is petitioned for in tradition.

Such is grace: The divine gives to us without reference to whether or not we deserve it. The Presence accompanies us regardless of what we do. Our moments are everlastingly saved without any test of merit. So, what does change between God and us when we violate another? I believe the nature of the possibilities changes. In the moments after the accident, God could hardly continue to offer the same lure to remain alert and drive safely down the road. The entire constellation of realistic and relevant possibilities changes because the situation has radically shifted. God now offers lures to a young man who is injured and experiencing severe shock. Lures have shifted to the most primitve methods of survival.

Is this forgiveness? Yes, I affirm that it is, although not couched in the traditional language of *Kyrie Eleison:* "Lord, have mercy!" Ray is forgiven, if by that we mean that God remains steadfastly intimate, involved, and graceful.

Should Ray request forgiveness from God? This question deserves exploration. First, I am aware that this question would have sounded ridiculous throughout most of Christian history. Of course he must. It is mandatory and essential for his salvation, the very saving of his soul. When one is in right relationship with God, that is enough, one is well also. The great images of Christendom portrayed God as the king, lord, warrior, and judge, the all-knowing, the utterly powerful, totally controlling, fully righteous being. Simply being forgiven by such a God was sufficient and complete. Even the saving act of Jesus dying on the cross was spoken of in terms of "atonement," allowing all persons to be at one with the divine. It is only in our modern era that the concept of self-forgiveness emerged. As we became more secular, our focus shifted to our own assessment of ourselves as being central; persons accept themselves. My discussion will hope to blend the traditional and the modern understandings by addressing both God and person.

So, should Ray plead forgiveness before God? If it means that Ray speaks honestly from his depths about what he has done and how he feels about those actions, then, Yes. Such intimate conversation between Ray and the Sacred One certainly enhances the depth and quality of their relationship. In traditional terms this purging of soul was called confession, reflecting the adage, "Confession is good for the soul."

Will God be any different with Ray because he utters these words? Only in the sense of gaining a more deeply satisfying relationship. God will know that Ray feels deep remorse and regret for harming a beloved, a part of God's cherished creation. God will delight that Ray is joining God in a loving empathy for creation. God will be comforted also by Ray's sense that God, empathizing with each of the family members, was deeply injured, too. God will rejoice that Ray feels the pain that God feels. The delight might be partly captured in the divine words of pleasure spoken in the Hebrew Bible: "Behold, my faithful servant Job."

Ray's most difficult task is not the struggle with whether or not God has forgiven him, but rather the struggle of accepting that God has forgiven him. Paul Tillich's famous sermon title, though preached from a differing vision of God, expresses the need: "Accept that you are accepted." Traditionally the problem was framed, "How can I even begin to forgive myself until I am assured that God has forgiven me?" Truly, such a question emerges from a different worldview than the one I embrace. I express a reversal: "Knowing that you are accepted by God, will you accept yourself?"

Whether guided by a religious or secular understanding of life, Ray's journey is one of increasingly accepting and forgiving himself. This journey is easier when guided by the newer vision of the divine. There is a naturalness that flows from vision to acceptance. Yet, even here the decision to accept himself will be made time and again, even under the best of circumstances. Overhearing a person's unkind word about the accident, the next event in the legal proceedings, a recurring nightmare displaying the horror, a critical voice from within, all will require renewing the decision to join God in accepting himself. That oft repeated decision is encouraged by the basic trust that he is accepted by the One who calls all beloved.

It is to be hoped that along the pathway Ray has avoided certain side-tracks that could have been left him frozen, imprisoned, and trapped. He could have been continually looking backward, being trapped in the past. He might have continued to avoid his own responsibility for the accident, seeking someone or something else to blame. He could have veered in the opposite direction of self-blame by naming himself a "loser" who is basically bad, completely unsalvageable, and totally irresponsible. He might have concluded that his life was ruined, leaving no hope for his future other than to just get through each day. Often these labels are accompanied by self-condemnations merged with the necessary prescriptions of drugs and alcohol to soothe the psychological pain. He might never have stopped running long enough to think, a radical form of denial of the event. Most likely a combination of these sidetracks would be chosen.

While all of these endeavors would seriously impair Ray, I would point out again that an extreme danger built into all of them is to block out any of the divine whispers that are offered to lead him to a life more broad and deep, more enriching and satisfying. Divine whispering does not stop when deflected or blocked, but the nature of the options offered must be realistic, hence increasingly limited. I wonder about the young woman who might fall in love with Ray or the young men who have been his circle of friends. A limited relationship appears the best that might be created, placing Ray in a sad and lonely way of life.

I hope that Ray was able to safely travel the pathway to self-forgiveness and continue to blossom in his youthful life. Perhaps his steps might be lighter, the pathway smoother, because of naming his offense, accepting responsibility for it, facing the consequences of society, harmonizing the inner voices with the divine voice, and accepting that the Lover of the Universe continues to encircle him with grace.

A PERSONAL PRAYER OF CONFESSION

I am grateful for Your presence,
    for Your knowing me in my totality,
    for Your having known me from my conception,
    for accompanying me through each stage of growth,
    for calling my name long before I knew Yours,
    for placing within my heart Your heart's desires,
    for ever encircling me with Your grace.
I am thankful for Jesus Christ,
    and those who have followed him,
    through whom I have come to know You.
I know that even now You continually engage with me,
    and that I address You in times of need.
That You repeatedly call, lure, and whisper
    even when I do not listen.
That You call all beloved,
    including those I call adversary and enemy.
That You cry and suffer with those
    whom I wish to safely ignore.
That You are in the midst of conflicting peoples,
    a burden that I do not wish to bear.
That You are friend to the oppressed,
    those strangers I have never fully known.
That You love and nurture the garden,
    while I often take it for granted.
That You cherish all creatures great and small,
    while I value them for what they can offer me.
That Your vision encompasses the universe,
    while I see occasionally beyond my community.
That You revere all of life,
    while I am continually selecting.
That You see me as a transforming person,
    as I tiptoe most cautiously on that journey.
I fervently desire the rays of Your sacred light, thereby
    to remain open to your caring persuasion,
    to risk, though frightened, on behalf of grace,
    to present myself authentically to others,

to know my own story told honestly,
to deepen my intimate relationships,
to celebrate and rejoice in the ordinary,
to hold fast to hope though catastrophe hovers,
to accept my body just as it is today,
to live bountifully in this period of history,
to call beloved all whom You so name.
May Your heart's desires for me
and my heart's desires for me
blend into one,
as they did for Jesus Christ. Amen.

A Corporate Prayer of Confession

O Gracious One,
as we gather as Your community
we open our hearts to You.
How grateful we are for Your presence among us,
encircling and enriching our gathering.
We stand surrounded by the rich symbols of You
inherited from our forebears in the faith:
the book, the cross, the altar, the
baptismal font, the pulpit, the lectern,
the statuary, the stained-glass windows.
Our senses are flooded
by their stories of Your gracious presence,
and their responses to Your grace.
We remember their adventures with You,
their awesome accomplishments,
their acts of unlimited love,
their glaring neglect, and
their grievous errors.
And we acknowledge our similarity to them,
in both our responding to and avoiding Your call.
May we learn from both their errors and our own.
May we listen for who You would have us become,
becoming aware of
the particular persons who long for our touch,

the unique tasks that stand before us,
the challenging issues needing our attention.
May we open ourselves now to Your transformation
just as we have closed ourselves before.
May we be Your voice, hands, and feet,
in this place, in this time.
And may we lift our voices in prayer,
for Your universal community
undergirding those who are
Your voice, hands, and feet,
throughout Your beloved creation.
May we be so filled with the grace
of which Jesus Christ spoke
and from which he lived,
that we may be, in both word and deed,
the church of Jesus Christ. Amen.

10

Imagining God's Heavenly Community

The scene that we are about to enter is a total flight of imagination—a wild leap into the unknown. Though the preceeding eight stories have been based upon real events, they were ultimately fiction, composed to illustrate how a newer vision of God would understand the place of forgiveness in that situation. I offer this flight not because I delight in the speculation of a theological "science fiction," but to place some form of overarching conclusion to my understanding of forgiveness.

Most of the stories posed earlier ended with ambiguity, the final outcome unknown. Also, many times it would appear that the offenders "got off easy" without facing major consequences for their actions. Never was it stated that the "bad guy would get it in the end," have to "face his Maker," be given his or her "just deserts" later, or be judged at death or the Second Coming in the "great courtroom in the sky." Nor was it implied that revenge be left to God, following the admonition: "Vengeance is mine, says the Lord." Those omissions were not oversights, for none of those conclusions fit with the newer vision, as much as they may offer temporary relief to the unavenged victim. To speak to these issues, as well as to complete the entire mosaic of forgiveness, this concluding portrait is offered.

Perhaps only to bolster my own confidence, I do need to share that there is precedence in Christian tradition for such a venture. John of Patmos shared his "Revelation" of the final days of earth, Dante Alighieri left us a graphic travelog of hell as he walked the *Inferno,* and John Bunyan offered us the journey of Christian in *Pilgrim's Progress.* Indeed, today every cartoonist knows exactly what heaven looks like and who will greet us outside the Pearly Gates. I hope that the diorama that I create will be more grounded and thoughtful than these comic repetitions of a questionable theology.

I begin by stating the central questions clearly before offering my own answers. Do persons who violently offend others have any consequences beyond that which our legal system and society mete out to them? Do those who fully and willfully intended to deprive an innocent person of something precious ever suffer in any mea-sure as much as the victim? Does God punish the offender? Is there any form of divine judgment that befalls the violator of another? Has grace no teeth? I intend to answer these questions!

The first brush strokes splashed on the canvas will illustrate one picture, not two: heaven, not heaven and hell. My conviction is that the newer vision of God offers us only one—a heavenly commu-nity. I am encouraged to feature one outcome for our lives, since neither the flaming, or sometimes freezing, hell or the Renaissance pastoral scenes of heaven attract me.

Three images do speak to me: heavenly community, heavenly banquet, and person-in-community. One might be able to create one integrated and unitary picture from these symbols. The central image, however, is that which has guided this entire endeavor: God as intimate, persuasive, and graceful. I assume that there is no reason to believe that these qualities change at our death and ensuing en-trance into the heavenly community. Extrapolating from these fea-tures, a picture may begin to take shape. It is necessary, however, to make clear my assumptions underlying this entire creation.

I assume that we survive physical death, our personal identity as individuals is retained, memory of our past earthly life is available, our creative process of experiencing continues in a new form, our awareness of other persons and God is present, and continuing trans-formation of our personhood occurs. More simply, we live beyond death in some form that allows us to know who we are, to remember, to be aware in the present, and continue growth. We are not simply winged and static harp players.

Now I make another assumption, which is a great leap of faith. The empathy that we naturally and normally experience in earthly life will be intensified as we enter the heavenly community. We feel with others now, shedding tears when a friend cries, delighting with the joy of another person, tensing with the frightened child, and furrowing our brow with one who is worrying. I am proposing that the experience of empathy here and now will be transformed, fulfilled, completed, expanded, broadened, and deepened. Among all these attempts to describe the change, I will choose the word "intensify," knowing full well that no word fully captures the actual experience.

I am further assuming that it is God's grace that undergirds all empathy. God's grace toward us gives rise to God's empathy for us and promotes empathy between us and others as well as between us and ourselves. While we may know intellectually that God's grace encircles us in every moment, we experience that grace fully only on limited occasions. While we may know cognitively that we are accepted by God in each moment, again we experience such acceptance only at times. I affirm that empathy that is partial during our earthly experiences becomes complete and fulfilled in the heavenly community.

My brush strokes create a vision of the heavenly community as encircling grace, a deep reservoir of grace, a massive star flaming with grace, light rays of grace emanating outward, a field of force totally entwined by grace. How can one speak of the unspeakable? How can one even imagine the heavenly community of God? Which inadequate words can begin to encompass this heavenly realm? Whatever the awesome character, it is into this sphere that we are called, surrounded by accepting grace and lured toward full transformation.

In many traditions it is the guardian angel who guides and accompanies us into the heavenly realm. With the image of God as king enthroned at some distant location, angels were necessary as messengers and as guardians, winging their way between the terrestrial and the celestial spheres. However, if God is truly intimate with each of us throughout living, dying, and beyond death, then it is God rather than an angel who leads us onward.

I am proposing also that everyone enters the community of God and that this process may or may not be a pleasant experience. However it may be, the entering person is empowered by the surrounding grace to face whatever need be encountered in the community.

Imagine with me an entrance. In whatever form they may be, a newly entering person comes into the presence of an individual whom he or she violated in life. The offending person will feel intensified empathy with the offended, something that most likely was not felt at the time of the offense. The offender will feel exactly the pain that he or she inflicted upon the other. If he hit her, he will feel the full impact of that blow upon himself. If she betrayed his trust, she will feel the full psychological pain of that betrayal that he endured. If he murdered her, he will feel the massive force that he inflicted upon her body.

Herein are powerful consequences of the harmful act, not simply those meted our during one's lifetime. These consequences are unavoidable. God is unable to prevent those consequences, just as those earlier consequences during earthly existence could not be avoided. To imagine that emnity, hatred, deceit, distance, and hiding may exist in God's heavenly community is incompatible with both who God is and the quality of the community surrounding God.

If unresolved between the persons or groups during their earthly existence, the resolution takes place here. The beginning of the unfulfilled reconciliation takes place in the first encounters. We may consider that Marcella fully experiences Anthony's range of feelings when she concluded their marriage. But just as fully, Anthony comes to a new awareness of Marcella's gradual pain of neglect. Juan feels the experience of Rosa as she is slapped in the face, blocked from leaving a room, and pushed over in her chair. Fred feels the innumerable moments of physical and psychological pain of Rachel from the early sexual abuse and his ensuing denial.

Accompanying this empathy is understanding, remorse, and regret, the beginning of a mutual reconciliation between them. The traditional concept for these experiences is repentance, a turning around. The offender comes to know in experience, not simply theory, that which the offended endured. The remorse and regret are intensified as the offending person comes to understand that the Graceful

One felt the same pain as the victim. Not only was the victim hurt; God was hurt in exactly that same form.

I am reminded of the words of the returning prodigal son spoken to his father: "Father, I have sinned against heaven and before you."(Luke 15:18) The need for the primary apology and forgiveness is twofold, to the victim and to the One who empathized with that victim. In fact, there are usually many more than two, for there were family, friends, acquaintances, neighbors, and community members surrounding the offended one. All were victimized to some degree by the act against the one to whom they were related. Coming into the presence of those surrounding persons will bring a host of empathic feelings to the offender, with accompanying remorse. The web is large around each person, which means that many strands are shaken, distorted, and broken. Nonetheless, it is possible for the offender to face this web of persons when undergirded by God's intimacy, persuasion, and grace.

That which did not occur during their earthly experience is persuaded and prompted by the intense grace flowing from the presence of God. Grace permeates the community; grace is the fundamental reality within which the community exists. God neither commands nor forces reconciliation, for such would be to change the basic character of God. Grace is as grace has always been, fully available, now intensified, just as empathy is fully present, now intensified. I find this continuity exceedingly important, for otherwise we believe in one kind of God during our lifetime and another upon our death. The loving one becomes the judging one. Intimacy continues, persuasion continues, grace continues, intensified but not changed.

I have imagined the entrance into the heavenly community by famous or infamous figures: Mohandas K. Gandhi, Adolf Hitler, Mother Teresa, Jim Jones, Albert Schweitzer, Genghis Khan, Francis of Assisi. I can imagine for the entering persons, depending upon their earlier relationships, that the scene might be one of jubilant rejoicing, horrendous pain, overpowering remorse, or triumphant homecoming. I cringe as I try to comprehend the horrible journey of an individual facing six million persons who died at one's command! The web around those murdered in the Holocaust magnify the numbers beyond belief—spouses, parents, children, grandchildren, friends, neighbors, and sensitive world citizens. Still, grace persuades all toward the transformation of being person-in-community.

Imagining the entrance of Mother Teresa is much easier. Her encounters were surely of a different order: gratitude, love, respect, and honor. The welling up and outpouring of those who have been touched by her gifts must have been full rejoicing and celebration. I rather expect that for most of us, the entering journey will be a mix of feelings, much dependent upon our earlier efforts to understand and reconcile with others.

The Persuasive One continues to lure, encourage, and affirm the struggle of the entering one to fully know and be fully known in the community, assisting that person to face, feel, regret, repent, reconcile, and transform beyond the denials and distortions of prior earthly life. The image of the heavenly banquet from Christian tradition offers meaning here. Inviting is the persuasive challenge: "The kingdom of heaven may be compared to a king who gave a wedding banquet for his son…" (Matthew 22:2). Banquet evokes a gathered celebration and so I think it will be, as transformations occur and satisfactions and pleasures accrue. I imagine dining encircled with and embraced by God's grace and characterized by increasingly full empathy among those gathered. There persons see face to face, know totally, and feel completely. I wonder if we will dance!

The images of heavenly community, heavenly banquet, and person-in-community are evocative, urging us to expand our imagination beyond its usual limits. Influenced by them, I have placed some brush strokes on the canvas and invite others to pick up a brush and revise or enrich the scene. I smile at the vast gulf between my images and those described by Dante in his journey through the inferno. There each person was trapped in some unbearable torture suitable for the heinous, sinful, and evil acts performed in their earthy life. Revenge is accomplished there, justice is served there; however, grace is spoken here.

If not fully answered by implication by now, allow me to directly respond to the questions raised earlier. Yes, there are consequences to offenders beyond those exacted during earthly existence. We must face those whom we have offended. Yes, there is suffering in just the same measure as our victim suffered. No, there is no judgment or punishment intentionally inflicted on offenders. Consequences unfold, but not punishment. No, grace does not have teeth in the sense of avenging forceful action, but is rather a reservoir of awesome power. Grace is the most powerful force in this world and the world to come!

FINALLY RESOLVED—FULLY FREE

I long to be free,
so that
    I can recall my past without restraint,
    reciting my own story just as it was,
    having resolved my differences
    with others who shared my history.
No longer fearing an inner calling back
    to events that feel unfinished.
Possessing no need to be embarrassed,
    regretful, hurt, sad, or angry
    as I remember events and persons.
No longer using my precious energy
    struggling with that which is done.
Accepting actions just as they were.
    I yearn for my memory to be clear!
    I desire that my past be resolved!

I long to be free,
so that
    I can allow my thoughts to soar,
    to consider possible futures for myself.
To open to the whispers of grace,
    to stand with arms outstretched,
    ready to embrace the new and
    walk paths toward enrichment
    that I am offered in each moment.
I yearn for my imagination to be clear!
    I desire unbounded, unlimited vision!

I long to be free,
so that
    I can feel all that now encircles me,
    receiving that which is out there

without distortion or denial
as a protective part of me.
Discerning what is actually present
from what I wish were there.
Hearing even that which is threatening,
knowing that which is mystifying,
feeling that which is genuine,
embracing both tragedy and celebration.
Taking in the entirety of the web.
I long for my empathy to be deep!
I desire for my understanding to be wide!

Alas,
I am not fully free today
for my past bears remnants of
relationships not yet resolved.
My potential futures hover before me
distorted by my own limits and fears.
My present universe of relationships
is incomplete and shallow.
Nevertheless,
I am nurtured by the hope that Grace
will lure me forward,
however resistant I may be,
into continuing transformation
so that
I may be finally resolved,
fully free!

Afterword

I wish now to highlight the uniqueness of the vision that underlies the paths to forgiveness explored in this book.

Forgiveness in a relational universe is unique in that all are affected by any event in the cosmos. Forgiveness is a process for everyone, not just the specifically injured.

I know of no other model of forgiveness that would ask the offended to reconsider the way that life works, by affirming that we do not have guaranteed rights and freedoms to which we justly respond with hurt and anger when they are violated. We live with the guarantee of a Gracious Presence who is offering us grace in the form of empathic companionship, new possibilities, and ultimate saving. Grace alone offers us unshakeable hope.

The goal of forgiveness is to be open to God's graceful possibilities, not blocked by our intense anger, hurt, or vengefulness. Like a tree planted by a stream, we need to remain open to the deep nourishment that the divine offers to us in each moment. To be cut off from this source is to lose the richness of life. Yes, forgiveness opens the relationships with others, but I find it fundamental for us to remain open to God. As we do, so we can be certain that we will be lured, persuaded, and called to invest in all whom God loves.

I affirm many paths to forgiveness, not simply one. The situation itself will often guide us as to which path, or combination of paths, will be most fruitful. Reconciliation is wonderful when possible; visualization is enriching when reconciling is not possible.

I point toward the heavenly community as the location of the final consummation of forgiveness. Mine is clearly a flight of fantasy but is consistent with the basic vision I affirm. God does not change character from the earthly to the heavenly dimension, but remains consistently present, offering grace. So many of our relationships are left incomplete in our lifetimes, so many injustices go unresolved. Thus, in the context of encircling grace, I affirm that the resolutions will occur.

The primary conditions from which we need to be rescued are separation and dividedness. This is not to deny the power of the profound feelings of hurt, anger, and vengefulness, but is to point to our blocked relationship with the divine source of grace. Reconciliation with the One who brings new healing possibilities is the primary goal of forgiveness. When this dividedness is bridged, then it is certain that there will be divine persuasion to heal the separation with our human family.

Finally, I have been surprised in my deliberations on forgiveness, for an experience of serendipity has come. I am saying something in these closing words that in the beginning I did not set out to write. My written words have taken on a life of their own and have spoken back to me in ways that I would not have expected. I have discovered that I need new terms with which to describe our relationship with God.

Christian tradition has always joined our confession of sin and request of forgiveness in our prayer to God. We state our wayward ways, cry out our remorse, vow from henceforth to follow the divine leading, and plead with God to forgive us. Kyrie, eleison! "Lord, have mercy!" The Christian community has named itself the forgiven and forgiving community. I am touched and moved by both the confession and the name of my community, yet I am discovering them to be inconsistent with my vision of God.

If, in fact, God is always intimate with us, ever offering new enriching possibilities, and saving everlastingly the moments we have just created, then in asking for forgiveness we are pleading for that which we already have and cannot lose. That relationship cannot be taken from us, for whether we wish it or not, or are aware of it or not, it is the nature of God to provide those forms of grace.

Traditionally that which we fervently desire from forgiveness is manifold: God will return to us, God will search for us and seek us out, God will close the wide chasm that our sin has created between us, God will cherish us, God will look favorably upon us, and God will continue to desire the very best for us. My vision affirms that we never lose these qualities, and cannot by our actions lose them. The intimate, persuasive, and gracious One continues steadfastly being who God is. The particular possibilities that God can realistically offer to us may be radically affected by our actions, but the divine presence remains ever embracing.

I compare it with praying an invocation, which I have done many times, asking that God be present, when God is always present. To ask for God's presence or to ask for God's forgiveness are both unneeded, for both are already a gift to us.

I affirm that we need only confession, leaving the rest of the action to God. Such confession is an authentic statement to God that we have not been infused by or alligned with God's heart's desires for both us and creation. We have not lived out of the divine vision. In this manner I affirm traditional modes of confession: an awareness that our desires are not God's, our actions have harmed both creation and God; contrition about where we have wandered; and a new decision to be open and responsive to God.

Following our confession, I would suggest stating a thanksgiving rather than a request for forgiveness. "We are grateful that You are always merciful to us, that from Your depth of knowing us You steadfastly offer us grace without condition."

In accordance with this approach, it delights me that when the prodigal returns home, his welcoming parent interrupts the conclusion of the son's prepared speech: "Treat me like one of your hired hands."(Luke 15:19b). He did, however, have opportunity to confess: "I have sinned against heaven and before you."(Luke 15:21). He was not able, at least in some scriptural versions of this story, to tell the parent how to respond. I wonder if this might serve as a model for us. We need not tell God how to respond to the genuine outpouring of our hearts, nor need we ask for what we already have.

Those prerogatives belong to God.

In light of these thoughts, I am finding it much more fruitful to speak of God as "gracing" us rather than "forgiving" us. Forgiveness may well be a meaningful term to use for our relationship with others in the human family. The language of grace may well belong only to God.

> Thanks be to God
> who is ever encircling us
> with grace!